PILGRIMAGE OF THE HEART

FINDING YOUR WAY BACK TO GOD

PILGRIMAGE OF THE HEART

FINDING YOUR WAY BACK TO GOD

BILL HENEGAR

Library of Congress Cataloging-in-Publication Data

Henegar, Bill, 1936-
Pilgrimage of the heart: finding your way back to God / Bill Henegar.
p. cm.
ISBN 0-89900-725-2
1. Jesus Christ–Passion 2. Jesus Christ–Resurrection. 3. Jesus Christ–Passion–Meditations. 4. Jesus Christ–Resurrection–Meditations. 5. Meditations. I. Title.
BT431 H45 1995
232.96–dc20 94-41727
CIP

For my mother, Ruth,

a pilgrim whom I have tried to follow

ACKNOWLEDGMENTS

There are many individuals who helped and encouraged the writing of this book, to whom heartfelt words of thanks are due, yet completely insufficient.

Twenty years ago, Silas Shotwell took me to an oasis in the middle of Portland, Oregon, and showed me a path that wound through a beautiful stand of trees, flowers and shrubs. It was my first view of the Way of the Cross. I guess I didn't think much about it at the time, but then, many years later, I found the Way again in another place. This path was different in appearance but embodied the same meaning and content. That rediscovery of the Way has blessed my life with renewal and refreshment. So, I am grateful to Silas for setting me on this special journey.

Regarding the writing of the book, F. LaGard Smith and Jerry Rushford, both professors at Pepperdine University, were invaluable to its completion and promotion. They had confidence, perhaps even when I wavered. More than he will ever know, I appreciate LaGard calling me from his cottage in England to tell me that he was touched by the manuscript. Then for months, he helped me through the publishing maze. And Jerry, always a loyal friend, not only added his excellent suggestions, but apparently saw something in the manuscript that led him to volunteer to promote the book as if it were his own. Both of these are true brothers in the Lord, and I owe them much.

I am also grateful for my friend and associate, Joyce Hutchison, whose proofreading, enthusiasm and assurance were crucial. She often kept me moving forward in the project. So many others have blessed my life in various ways before and during the writing of the book, particularly Morris Womack, Billie Silvey, Shirley Roper, and Sue Gamboa. It made me aware that, in the last analysis, nearly nothing in life is ever a solo venture.

Of course, my wife, Laurette, was and is a source of unending love and support. I am very much aware that anything I accomplish or hope to ever accomplish in life is, for the most part, because of her partnership and sacrificial spirit. If the words in this volume are mine, they are hers, just as surely.

Finally, I am indebted to the gracious hosts of Serra Retreat for providing a special path for my own weekly pilgrimages. And I remember the countless and nameless "little brothers" of Francis who, centuries before Serra Retreat, kept the Way of the Cross from being overgrown by the weeds of neglect and forgetfulness. Their labors have not been in vain. At least one man, near the turn of the twenty-first century, discovered the Way that they protected and perpetuated . . . and entered into it.

Bill Henegar

CONTENTS

11 *Preface*

15 *Prologue:* THE WAY

19 *Chapter One:* THE END OF JUDGMENT

29 *Chapter Two:* LABORING WITH WOOD

41 *Chapter Three:* LEARNING TO STAND AGAIN

53 *Chapter Four:* A VESSEL FOR GOD'S USE

65 *Chapter Five:* WALKING IN HIS STEPS

79 *Chapter Six:* LISTEN TO THE ALARM

91 *Chapter Seven:* A TIME TO DIVEST

103 *Chapter Eight:* BEARING THE MARKS

113 *Chapter Nine:* LIFTED UP

129 *Chapter Ten:* CHALLENGE OF OBEDIENCE

143 *Chapter Eleven:* A BROKEN LOCK

151 *Chapter Twelve:* POWER IN THE MORNING

163 *Epilogue:* REMEMBERING THE GLORY

167 *Notes*

PREFACE

There are times when I'm anxious to reach that special place called "home" . . . because relaxation awaits there. And familiarity. And freedom to be myself.

So I choose the route that takes me home the quickest and devour the road.

But at other times, I have a different longing: a desire to travel far from where I'm comfortable, see new sights, meet new people. Just wander and drift and catch a glimpse of what's on the other side.

The short way is, by far, the usual way I approach my life. But it usually isn't very fulfilling. There's a hunger in my soul for more than the quickest way to ease and entertainment.

Long ago, the Teacher in the book of Ecclesiastes said, "There is a time for everything, and a season for every activity under heaven" (3:1). I've found that there are times to rush, and there are also seasons to wander in deep contemplation and exploration. In this book, I invite you to join me on a special journey that moves away from the fast track and takes us home the long way

– home to God by way of the cross.

My premise is that we take the short route much too often in our hurried and overcrowded lives. With our "sound-bite" attention spans. And our "schedule-for-success" agendas.

The pilgrimage we now begin leads through dark places as well as light, through places we often try to avoid. I find it interesting that our *aversions* sometimes produce the very things we hope to escape. For example, all the pain relievers, tranquilizers, alcohol and drugs people consume – all the entertainment, television, sports and recreation into which people rush – fail to make society whole. The fact is, there is more pain, disappointment, fear and death now than many of us can ever remember, and even though we avoid these things with all our strength, they pursue and haunt us.

Could it be that too many shortcuts, quick fixes and instant successes have stolen away our joy, our character – even our sanity? Perhaps we are unwise in trying to circumnavigate the difficult and even disastrous aspects of our lives. After all, the sun seems to shine the brightest and is appreciated the most after the dark night of the storm.

A few years ago, I discovered a little pilgrimage that has become very special to me. Thousands have traveled it before me, although there are probably fewer pilgrims on the winding road now than in the past, because shortcuts sell well today. Regardless of that, I highly commend the journey to you.

The vantage points at which we pause and reflect on this journey are meaningful to me because of my experiences at a retreat center in Malibu, California. There, a special path has been provided that winds along the edge of a hill overlooking the famous Malibu Colony, a seaside community of fame and affluence.

The beautiful mansions and beautiful people below

provide a rather sharp contrast to the garden on the hill that symbolizes the way of humility. Spaced along the path are a number of sculpted scenes of the way of the cross. I've made it my practice to walk along the pathway at least once a week, if at all possible, and the little journeys have enriched my life immeasurably.

This particular "exercise" is much more than a stroll in the sun with a view of the Pacific Ocean over one's shoulder. In the mind, heart and soul of the pilgrim, it is a reenactment of those eternity-shaping events that take us from the condemnation of Jesus to his death – and finally to his spectacular vindication as he stepped from the tomb into the sunlight of life.

As I walk the path, I pause to meditate and pray at each marker, and I consciously try to *identify* with Jesus at that point along the way. Somehow, the meaning of the cross looms larger and larger as I struggle alongside him. The resurrection shines more brilliantly as I meditate on the glorified Lord of Life.

My prayer is that these pages will serve as an introduction to a practice that you'll embrace for a lifetime . . . until you embrace him, the one who walked the long, lonely road to Golgotha and glory.

Bill Henegar
Thousand Oaks, California
October 3, 1994

Prologue

THE WAY

"Oh! for a closer walk with God,
A calm and heav'nly frame,
A light to shine upon the road
That leads me to the Lamb!"

— William Cowper, 1772
Olney Hymns

My favorite time of the year is spring. No matter how often I experience it, I'm always astounded to see vibrant green grass there beneath the ice and snow as they melt. The swollen buds and blossoms, the awakening flora and fauna are a reaffirmation of life itself. It is the season of resurrection.

I think it may be significant that we really have no idea in which season Jesus was born. We all love the family warmth of Christmastime, but we know that Jesus almost certainly wasn't born in December – or even in the winter. But we do know *exactly* when Jesus was crucified and resurrected, because it is dated by the Feast of Passover in the Jewish calendar and is very carefully specified. Passover was and is in springtime. And somehow I do not believe it is coincidental that Jesus rose to life in the season of rebirth.

Christians continually live in resurrection, in the springtime of the Spirit. At least that is the idea of spiritual life. But in reality, it is not always so. You and I sometimes slip into discouragement and depression, our faith grows weak and our spirits fail.

The question is, what do we do when the chilly winds of autumn come? What happens when the ice of spiritual winter entombs us and we are immobilized by despair?

I believe that is the time to remember that there is a *way back to the springtime* of our faith – a way that is both ancient and ever new. And, like the spring of the year, it is a refreshing, reviving, and renewing life-force.

Think about a "way." It can be a simple path or a thoroughfare. A route that leads to some destination, distant or nearby. A way also is a possibility, an answer, a solution. More broadly, it's a manner of living or an entire philosophy.

Ways can be joyful, sorrowful, tedious – sometimes even terrifying – but nearly always, they are intriguing. Because they stretch out from where we are to where we've never been – or where we want to be, should be, can be. They slip around bends, rise over mountains, proceed uncharted through the seas, and disappear beyond the horizon.

Long ago, Jesus spoke of a very special way when he said, "I am the way and the truth and the life. No one comes to the Father except through me" (John 14:6).

He calls us to himself because he *is* the way of life – the way *to life*. His timeless teachings are profound and revolutionary, pointing us toward the only truly fulfilling life. But the spiritual instructions of Jesus are only part of the way.

It may surprise you to learn that we actually have access to the world of the spirit – that realm we call heaven – *through the body of Jesus*. In other words, his *body* also is the way of life.

The book of Hebrews tells us, "Therefore, brothers, since we have confidence to enter the Most Holy Place by the *blood of Jesus, by a new and living way opened for us through the curtain, that is, his body* . . . let us draw near to God with a sincere heart in full assurance of faith . . ." (Hebrews 10:19-22).

It's because of the sacrificial way Jesus walked that we have access to heaven through his body. Somehow in God's plan, the body of Jesus became a passageway to life for us. So, our way to heaven is through the way of the cross of Christ.

We shouldn't be surprised that the way of life is intricately tied to pain and sacrifice. The birth of every human life is a parable: it is accompanied by the pain – and by the blood – of a mother who provides her child with a "way" of transition from one world (the womb) to another (the outside environment). The mother's body is that passageway to the baby's "new world."

The key to the way we now walk, and to the entire Christian life, is *identification* with Jesus. In the coming chapters I hope to impress upon you how completely Jesus identified with us in our weakness. But just as he identified with us, we must be ready to identify with him. When we do, we become one with him in mind, in heart, in purpose, in life, in death, in glory. Paul wrote, "Set your minds on things above, not on earthly things. For you died, and your life is now hidden with Christ in God. When Christ, who is your life, appears, then you also will appear with him in glory" (Colossians 3:2-4).

Real faith is identification. My life must be hidden with Christ in God, so that "for me to live is Christ," as Paul put it. That means sharing in the victory of the risen Lord; but it also means sharing in the death of the suffering Savior. Being one with Jesus includes walking the way of the cross with him from start to finish – from condemnation to crucifixion – then continuing on with him to share in his triumphal resurrection.

There are steps along nearly every way. Usually they appear as landmarks, signposts or points of interest that mark our progress. In the same way, it's possible to identify specific markers along the way of the cross – places to ponder the dramatic events that carried Jesus to the profound conclusion of his earthly mission and the exalted position God gave him.

The chapters that follow introduce us to an exercise, if you will, a practice or pilgrimage that can enrich our lives immeasurably if we continue it through the years. I'm suggesting that the very center of our Christian lives must be the cross of Christ, and we must visit that center again and again – weekly, even daily if we're able. For the way of the cross leads to the thing we need most: life!

The historical way of the cross is the eternal taproot of Christianity, from which it draws life and strength. And I hope you'll discover that the power to believe and the power to live in the Son flow from Jesus and his way of sorrows. The key is identification with the Savior.

From sermons, Bible classes, study fellowships and personal devotions, you probably know the way from beginning to end. There are no surprises. But I've come to believe that a great measure of grace is available to those who patiently and repeatedly identify with the shame of the cross as they march toward new life.

There's a way that seems easy – like a comfortable, eight-lane interstate highway – but it leads to desolation. There is another way that seems hard – like a winding, treacherous mountain road – but it leads to glory. And that is the way we now walk.

Chapter One

THE END OF JUDGMENT

"I'll be judge, I'll be jury," said cunning old Fury;
"I'll try the whole cause, and condemn you to death."

– Lewis Carroll, 1865
Alice's Adventures in Wonderland

It would make sense to begin our pilgrimage in the garden of Gethsemane, that poignant place of prayer where, one might argue, the victory was really won. Or perhaps it would be appropriate to begin at that moment when Jesus "set his face toward Jerusalem" and the task he would accomplish there. In fact, there's even a sense in which it would be logical to begin our journey in Bethlehem, at the birth of Jesus. Because he was born in order to die a substitutionary death and be raised for you and me.

However, in the pilgrimage that's before us now, we'll begin with that moment when Jesus is condemned to be nailed to a Roman cross.

The Journey Begins

The agonizing hours of prayer in the garden, deep into the night, are over. The aching hours of interrogation have ended. The sham of a trial before the high court is finished. The vain attempt by the Roman governor, Pontius Pilate, to release Jesus on a technicality has failed. The flogging has not satisfied the thirst of the Jews for Jesus' blood.

Normally law-abiding people, who ought to be home in bed or just rising to go about their work, have been up most of the night. They've been joined by drifters and panhandlers. And the haters of Jesus who fear the loss of their positions of influence have whipped them all into a frenzied mob. Louder and more agitated they become. Eyes are wide with hate and destructive energy, red with impending violence. Like caged lions at feeding time, their carnivorous cry is, "Take him away! Crucify him, crucify him!" The descendants of the people who once had no king but Yahweh God now cry out, "We have no king but Caesar!" (John 19:15).

And so the moment comes. Reaching back into his memory, the old apostle John visualizes that terrifying, confusing and tumultuous moment and writes simply, "Finally Pilate handed him over to them to be crucified" (John 19:16).

The decision is made, and there's no turning back. The disciples of the carpenter from Nazareth have known him for three brief, shining years. Now the electrifying days of teaching and healing, of touching and loving – of truly living for the first time – are over. They have come to a disillusioning, ignominious end. Most of those who pledged their lives to the Messiah have fled like frightened children.

The conclusion is now in sight; the last chapter of the brilliant story will be closed on an ugly little hill outside of the city of God . . . or so it would seem.

Stand here, then, at this first step on our journey. Don't rush on. There's plenty of time to ponder, to grapple with what it all means. Time enough to see the entire drama unfold . . . to see the depths of man's folly and the unimaginable heights of God's wisdom.

There he is . . . there, planted on the judgment pavement – this Jesus of Nazareth. But his feet aren't planted too solidly. His knees are unstable, weakened from the tedium and trauma of an endless night. So recently he was hardy and strong. He is, after all, a working man – a tradesman, a carpenter. He has none of the pallor of the court politicians. His hands aren't smooth like the tax collectors or the scribes. He's used to long hours of heavy labor, tiring days of travel by foot. But even the strongest aren't prepared for the physical toll of this kind of contempt and rejection and such cruel abuse. Now, to crown the horrible affair, the decree of death on a Roman cross is given.

The sentence is immutable and immediate. Jesus won't be placed on "death row" where he has the possibility, however slight, of a stay of execution. This isn't the era of the right of appeal or commuted sentences. Life is cheap here in the first century A.D. In less than an hour, the death squad will arrive at "the place of the skull." And it will be done. The beautiful words that elevated every human being to the status of God's beloved, the touch that opened blind eyes and straightened twisted legs, the voice that called forth the dead and sent demons scurrying . . . everything will be over.

Gaze into the courtyard. Don't you see him there? His chin rests heavily on his chest. His eyes are swollen and closed; he opens them only occasionally to see if anything around him has changed. He is forcing his thoughts away from the immediate disgrace and pain to another place, a distant (yet near) realm where Someone waits – and weeps.

His face is red with welts raised by the hands of the Roman warriors who seem to enjoy torturing their gentle captive. The garment on his back is streaked with blood from the stripes they inflicted on him earlier. He weaves back and forth slightly, fighting for consciousness. But there's no need for medical attention; the risk of infection is unimportant, the loss of blood of no concern . . . for he has only a few hours to live.

For the first time, we notice that the small trickles of crimson that flow down his face and neck are not from the beating but from puncture wounds on his head. With great care not to prick their fingers, the soldiers have twisted spiny branches into a "crown."

And perhaps Jesus is thinking, "A day is coming when everyone, including you soldiers, will bow before a crown – not a garland of thorns, but a crown of blazing light! And you men will recognize the one who wears it."

The Creator is Judged

Listen. The last words of condemnation echo through the halls and settle on this gentlest of men, this one who is better than the sum total of all men. Listen to the pronouncements of weak and pompous people *condemning* the holiest who ever lived. Can you hear the sentence of death fall on the Author of Life, the very one who will return to judge the living and the dead?

If the scene were not so shameful, it would be laughable. Picture it if you will: pitiful little men, who deserve nothing but death, pulling themselves up on their tiptoes and proclaiming the Prince of Peace guilty and deserving of death! It is a scene where condemned *creatures* pass judgment on their own *Creator*.

Meanwhile, the sinless one stands in unfathomable patience. This Infinite One who has entered finiteness, who made all things including the very people who now sentence him, waits to suffer and die at the hands of his little creatures.

The irony is overwhelming. Imagine a tiny, molded clay pot rising up in ridiculous indignation to strike at the potter who molded it. And here before us, the mighty Potter patiently submits to the insults and the evil treatment of the little vessels he has made.

Jesus is condemned to death – the scandal of the thought offends our pride and confounds our logic if we really try to ponder it. This battered and sorrowful man before us is, indeed, God fitted into the form of a man. He is, indeed, humbling himself, bending himself low under the sentence of sinful humanity. How it can be, we can't fully know. But one day it will be made plain to us, and our astonishment and praise will echo through eternity.

As we see Jesus standing there in pain and weakness, it's tempting to cast all our frustration and anger on the Romans and the Jews who dared to carry out this greatest travesty of justice in history. But as we walk the steps of Jesus, we come to realize instinctively that *we were there!* We participated in the verdict of that cold, stone judgment hall. We were there on the portico as the governor paraded him out before the mob. If that particular crowd hadn't judged him, then other fallen creatures – or we ourselves – would have. That, after all, is why he had to die . . . because we are who we are: people filled with evil, people in desperate need of forgiveness.

So, before we point an accusing finger at those first century judges and absolve ourselves of the world's most heinous crime, we should remember that Jesus tolerated the judgment of people because there was no other way to save people. All of us – from Adam on down to the last baby who will be born – can have hope through this strange plan that is now unfolding before us.

Is there a lesson to be learned as Jesus stands under the condemnation of the wisest and most learned men of his day? It is chilling to remember the words he spoke to the multitudes on the mountainside. "Do not judge, or you too will be judged," he said. "For in the same way you judge others, you will be judged, and with the measure you use, it will be measured to you" (Matthew 7:1,2).

Judgment Under Judgment

At this first step on the way to the cross, I believe judgment itself is brought under judgment. I'm convinced we're called to forsake judging one another – here, as we *begin* our journey to the cross.

But that's easier said than done. Because judging others is to us what alcohol is to the alcoholic. We seem to have a compulsion to judge others in order to establish our own worth. The remedy for our improper self-image is to rethink our individual situations, rather than to focus on and compete with others.

As I've walked the way of Jesus, I've noticed that Christianity – faith – begins with humility. Emptying ourselves, breaking our pride, is the first requisite for discipleship. We really can't learn much about spirituality until we admit our own sin and ignorance. When we consider and confess our spiritual poverty, then we find we haven't the status to judge another spiritual pauper.

We must learn that it's impossible to walk with Jesus in the journey to glory and continue to judge our brothers and sisters. Because they are not ours to judge; they belong to another. "Who are you to judge someone else's servant?" Paul asks. "To his own master he stands or falls. And he will stand, for the Lord is able to make him stand" (Romans 14:4).

Judging others is a natural tendency in us. Natural, but sinful. Perhaps it stems from the fact that we know we are weak and inadequate. We know we fail both ourselves and God, and so we project our dissatisfaction with ourselves onto others.

I've discovered that I'm the most critical of my wife, my children, my employer, my church – everyone and everything – when I'm the unhappiest with myself. I somehow try to cast my failings and frustrations onto them. I see them doing what I myself am doing or have done, and I judge them. Because in some twisted way, I apparently feel I can transfer my guilt. By pointing out their failures, I think I can diminish my own.

At other times I'm tempted to feel superior because I've succeeded in some way that another person hasn't. Maybe I've studied my Bible more, attended more church services or Bible classes, given more money to the church or other good causes. In subtle ways, I try to justify myself by comparing my actions with those of others. I think I'll be justified because someone else has failed: "At least I'm better than he is!"

But whether we are projecting our own guilt onto others or trying to justify ourselves, judgment is dead wrong. And we must flee from it.

This isn't to say that we will never have to make tough decisions and deal with sin in people's lives. But when that's the case, we must proceed with extreme care, with the purest of motives and with the Holy Spirit of God. Paul chastised the Corinthian Christians for allowing sin to run rampant in the church. He said, "It is actually reported that there is sexual immorality among you, and of a kind that does not occur even among pagans . . . ." Then he instructed them, "When you are assembled in the name of our Lord Jesus and I am with you in spirit, and the power of our Lord Jesus is present, hand this man over to Satan, so that the sinful nature may be destroyed and his spirit saved on the day of the Lord" (1 Corinthians 5:1,4,5).

The situation in Corinth was a very unusual and acute one, and it called for wise judgment. Our judgments are often of a different kind. They are based on "human standards" (John 8:15ff).

Dealing With Pride

Where do bitterness and hatred spring from? What's the source of gossip, slander, and even violence and murder? Don't these things arise from hearts that are filled with pride and judgment? When we prejudge and stereotype someone, when we presume to know a person's heart, when we think we possess wisdom in and of ourselves . . . we have begun the same thought processes that put Jesus on the cross. For that was the attitude of the enemies of our Lord.

However, when we walk the way of Jesus, much of the conflict we have with others fades away, beginning here at the first step of our journey. For how can we judge others and harden our hearts against them when we see Jesus standing here, judged by all men? How can we be so sure our judgments are just? God said he himself will judge all people, relieving us of that terrible responsibility. "There is only one Lawgiver and Judge, the one who is able to save and destroy. But you – who are you to judge your neighbor?" (James 4:12).

When we're brought face to face with the fact that it's *our own sins and judgments* that have brought Jesus here, then perhaps we'll finally cease our judging. Maybe when we envision the condemned Son of God waiting to die, we'll finally say, "Enough! No more judgments! Judgment belongs to God alone. Only he is great and wise enough to know the hearts of people."

And when others join in this resolve, then the healing of our churches, our schools, our workplaces and our nation will begin. Perhaps even the divisions between sincere believers in Christ will be healed.

Humility is the beginning of knowledge, of peace, of salvation. The very first thing Jesus said as he sat down to teach on the mountainside was, "Blessed are the poor in spirit." And that's the beginning place for a life that's committed to God.

Before we can proceed in the Christian life, we must humble ourselves. There's no other way. Before we can walk the way of the cross, we must acknowledge that we're not wise enough or great enough to judge others. We are God's servants, and we're not to judge other servants.

Submission

Here at this first step, Jesus also gives us a powerful example of submission to authority and to the sentence of death.

Though Pilate is corrupt and unjust, the Son of God submits to him as the lawfully appointed governor. Jesus puts himself under the power of the Romans and Jews because he knows that the Father is working through people and history to accomplish his will.

Perhaps we should ask, "If Jesus submitted to evil men even though he was the Son of God, how can we refuse to obey those who have authority over us?"

I remember one particularly trying time in my life when I thought I was being treated unkindly and unjustly. I struggled greatly and was very depressed. I sought help but found only a little sympathy. Finally, I turned the situation over to God and asked him to work through it for his glory. It became a turning point in my life. I honestly believe that God worked in that set of circumstances and has been glorified through them. If Jesus submitted to authority, how can I not obey those who have been placed over me?

Secondly, not only did Jesus submit to authority, he also submitted to death. No submission is easy, but this kind is especially difficult. Imagine what it was like for the Son, who was conscious of eternity and knew that he was the Author of life, to suffer the weakness and humiliation of death!

Most of us approach our physical lives as if they are

the only reality. But that is illusion. The earliest Christians understood what many of us seemed to have forgotten – the most terrible thing in life *is not* death . . . it is disobedience to God.

Sometimes our prayers betray us. They reveal our preoccupation with physical well-being rather than spiritual health and spiritual warfare. Certainly, we are taught to pray for the healing of the sick. But physical healing must never take precedence over spiritual realities. We have greater things in store for us than this present existence.

Jesus submits to Pilate and to death because he knows the source of true life. And we must keep our physical lives in proper perspective – because we identify with Jesus who is the author and sustainer of life. He knows there are things infinitely more valuable than a few more days on this earth. Jesus can stare into the fangs of death because he sees resurrection just beyond.

It's time to move on. The journey is just beginning, and terrible challenges lie ahead. But unspeakable joy also awaits us. Remember, our salvation lies in *identification* with our Master.

Jesus himself said, "A student is not above his teacher, nor a servant above his master. It is enough for the student to be like his teacher, and the servant like his master" (Matthew 10:24,25). If Jesus walked the way of the cross, how can we escape walking it with him? It's enough for us to be like our teacher and master, the one who died on a cross.

As we turn and move on, look a last time at the one standing in the hall of judgment. It is Jesus the carpenter, the rabbi from Nazareth – the Son of Man and the Son of God – the one who will die on a cross.

But glory lies on the other side of condemnation.

Chapter Two

LABORING WITH WOOD

"O Cross that liftest up my head,
I dare not ask to hide from Thee;
I lay in dust life's glory dead,
And from the ground there blossoms red,
Life that shall endless be."

– George Matheson, 1882

A soldier shoves the prisoner forward with a swift blow to the back, and the man half-stumbles down the flight of stone steps and into the courtyard of the Fortress Antonia. There, the death squad waits. Hardened warriors with blank stares surround the prisoner and stand motionless. Soon the sound of shuffling feet is heard within the bowels of the huge stone building, growing louder until two more prisoners emerge, led by soldiers into the courtyard. Brawny men appear, dragging heavy, roughly hewn wooden beams. They dump the crosses in between the executioners and the condemned men, then disappear.

Jesus is pushed forward, commanded to bend, put his shoulder under the beam and lift it. Then he is forced toward the gate of the courtyard. The two other condemned men are compelled to do the same.

It's fully light now. A new day has dawned . . . people throughout Judea are eating their breakfasts, tending to their animals, preparing for the day. Some are opening their shops, readying their services. Many are well into the hard work of the day – washing, plowing, planting, hammering. But none are taking up the burden of the men in the courtyard – a burden that will end the lives of those who bear it.

The Passover Lamb

Other soldiers clear a path through the crowd outside the gate of the garrison where the final judgment has taken place. Adjacent to this fortified castle, rebuilt by Herod the Great and named in honor of Mark Antony, is the temple compound. With the beginning of Passover near, the sacred place is a flurry of activity as priests and Levites prepare the lambs and other items for sacrifice.

Ironically, only a few hundred feet away, the True Passover Lamb sent by God is being prepared for sacrifice at exactly the same time – not by the priests, but by humanity as a whole. The True Lamb has been condemned to die, and now he lifts the ugly death instrument that will become an altar.

Grimaces distort the faces of the death squad soldiers. They make menacing gestures with their spears as they "fearlessly" move forward. But inwardly the soldiers are nervous, apprehensive, fearful of what could happen. They know how volatile the situation is, with the party of the radical Zealots always ready to capitalize on any emotional crisis. News of this "Nazarene thing" has spread all over Jerusalem, and the Zealot patriots could turn it into a confrontation between the Jews and the Romans. The Jews couldn't win in the long run, of course, but the soldiers know that their own lives are on the line. They couldn't control a full scale riot – a mob would tear them to bits. So they growl and swear and do their best to intimidate and bluff the people on the street.

What they don't understand is that patriotism is not

driving the passion of the crowd at all. The Jewish leaders have incited the people with religious bigotry, and typical of a seething mob, no one is thinking ahead. The crowd doesn't realize that eliminating Jesus won't help their cause in any way. When Jesus is dead, the Romans still will stand with their heel on the Jewish neck – the Holy City still will be a place of subjugated people. Only the Jewish establishment – the chief priests and religious leaders, the politicians, the collaborators and Roman puppets – will be satisfied by removing this gentle One who seems to be a threat to their power.

The Jews and the Romans have joined hands in an unholy alliance. They have conspired to rid the city – and the world – of Jesus. They are waging war against the Prince of Peace.

The soldiers push their shields ahead and swing their blades in vicious arcs. The crowd parts like the angry waves of the Red Sea in Moses' day . . . the death squad passes through the gate. Behind the procession, a Roman drummer takes up a slow, somber cadence. The hollow, rhythmic percussions echo through the street, disappear around corners. The orange-yellow glow of early morning that should bring hope for another day, instead brings a throbbing announcement of death. It's an eerie sight, a chilling sound.

Those who love to be the bearers of the latest news run ahead of the procession, announcing in every nook and cranny that the rabbi called Jesus is being taken to the place of execution. The message spreads with the speed of the choicest gossip, because nearly everyone in Jerusalem has heard of the prophet from Nazareth. After all, only five days ago the young preacher had come riding into the city like a visiting king . . . well, like a king of sorts. Instead of riding on a royal stallion, Jesus had ridden on the back of a donkey. Instead of regal robes, he had worn the simple garb of a Galilean. And instead of being greeted by the nobility and the privilege seekers of the city, he had been greeted by the ordinary people, those who lived in hope of seeing the promised Messiah.

Many of the same people who ran and gathered palm branches to spread on his path, who hurried to pick flowers to sprinkle on him as he passed – those same people now press through the throng to get a closer look at the death squad as it passes by.

"Are you *sure* it's the same man, the one we thought was the Messiah?" a young man is saying. "I can't believe it's the prophet who rode into the city with such celebration!"

"Yes, it's him," comes the reply. "I'm sure of it. His face is swollen, and his hair is all matted down . . . but I'd recognize him anywhere. It's that Jesus from Nazareth, alright."

"But he's a rabbi – a teacher of the Lord! He's not a murderer or a thief or even a Zealot," comes the incredulous response. "What could he have done to deserve this? Why would anyone want him dead?"

Someone overhears the conversation and offers an explanation. "Haven't you heard? This 'rabbi' of yours claims to be king of the Jews. Ha! Look at him – some king, wouldn't you say?! Where's his army? I'd enlist under a real king . . ." – he lowers his voice – ". . . to overthrow those Roman pigs" – and louder again – "but this man isn't the leader we're looking for. He should have stayed with his preaching in those country towns of Galilee instead of trying to pass himself off as a king here in the Holy City."

"But what if he really is the Messiah . . .?" the first man wonders out loud.

"A messiah who's executed before he even *begins* to free us? You must be joking!" the self-styled expert says gruffly.

Now the death squad is passing directly in front of us. The babble of the throng immediately drops to a muffled whisper – as if an invisible blanket has settled over it.

The three condemned men come into full view between the armor-laden soldiers, and there, near the front of the procession, is Jesus. Even the sour cynic and the itinerant "expert" grow quiet as they see his face up close. The central figure of the triumphal entry a few days ago is now the man of the bloody cross. He stumbles forward – each step a major effort. He labors for breath as a soldier prods him with the flat of his spearhead. And always there's the beating of the drum, like some ghastly heartbeat. The air hangs heavy with the smell of death.

Those along the way with tender hearts recoil at the scene. Their sense of fairness, decency and justice is offended. It takes little wisdom and intelligence to see that an innocent man is about to die.

The Carpenter

Jesus pauses, shifts the beam to his other shoulder, then moves forward again, one shuffling step at a time. The astute observer might notice that, even in this painful scene, there's a certain deftness in the way Jesus handles the wooden beam. Only a few remember that these are the hands and shoulders of a master carpenter who has handled many wooden beams. He has sawed and shaved and shaped wood into tables, chairs and cabinets. He has cut roof beams and lifted them into place. He's a man who is intimately acquainted with that rich, distinct texture and smell of wood.

As he labors now in a much different way under his wooden burden, we might ask, Did Jesus ever know or sense that wood – the substance of his earthly craft – would be the very medium through which he would die?

Did he guess that some anonymous carpenter would shape a wooden beam into an instrument of death upon which his fellow carpenter from Nazareth would hang?

John's gospel tells of the great humiliation: "So the soldiers took charge of Jesus. *Carrying his own cross,* he went out to the place of the Skull (which in Aramaic is called Golgotha)" (John 19:16b,17). The Son of Man is not allowed the dignity of a last walk through his beloved Jerusalem, striding upright as he should. Instead, he's treated as a valueless slave, compelled to bend beneath his burden, looking down at the paving stones rather than up to the sky. It's all part of the humiliation, part of the plan to demonstrate just who's in control.

That's a game we sometimes play, isn't it? The name of the game is "Who's in charge?" or "Who's got the power?" We see it daily – in the news, in our work-places, in our churches, in our homes. The strongest put the weakest in their "proper" place. Those with authority lord it over those without. But Jesus, though he has *all power,* takes his place with the weakest of us . . . as if he were as powerless as we sometimes are.

So he plods forward – head down, jaw set, teeth clenched in determination to walk the way of sacrifice. Every minute of the long ordeal seems to add to the weight he carries.

Stand now in this throng of people . . . the day is warm, though it's still early morning . . . and the press of the crowd makes it feel even warmer. Jesus pauses again to catch his breath, his chest rising and falling in rapid succession. We see him there . . . carrying his own cross.

No one will die in his place – not Barabbas, not anyone. And no one will carry his cross – none but the Cyrenean and even then, only part of the way. Jesus himself carries the wooden object to which he will be nailed.

Teaching Us to Follow

He seems to have known all along how it would be for him. And for his followers. He said,

> If anyone would come after me, he must deny himself and take up his cross daily and follow me. For whoever wants to save his life will lose it, but whoever loses his life for me will save it. What good is it for a man to gain the whole world, and yet lose or forfeit his very self? If anyone is ashamed of me and my words, the Son of Man will be ashamed of him when he comes in his glory and in the glory of the Father and of the holy angels (Luke 9:23-26).

He spoke these words long before this moment on the Way of Sorrows.

It wasn't a coincidence that Jesus discussed crosses with his disciples. Before the arrest and condemnation, before this moment on the streets of Jerusalem, he knew a cross was waiting for him. In a sense, he always carried a cross with him – not a golden, cross-shaped bauble hanging from a chain around his neck – but a sentence of death. While he went about doing good and teaching people the meaning of life, he knew it wouldn't be long until he was executed as a common criminal.

So, as we watch him carry his cross along the Via Dolorosa, we are seeing *our forerunner*, our model, our teacher. He's leading the way, demonstrating the courage, teaching us how to carry a cross . . . how to live with a sentence of death. How to be ready to die.

Who in their right mind wouldn't want to follow Jesus into an exciting and glorious new life? Who wouldn't want assurance that death is but a transition into an eternal adventure in the presence of God? Jesus says, "If anyone would come after me . . . ." And millions of people shout, "Yes! We'll come after you. We'll follow you into heaven!"

But he continues. "If anyone would come after me, *he must deny himself* . . . ." After a moment's thought, many decide, "Sure! I can do that. I can forget about 'me' for awhile and follow Jesus. Count me in!" Multitudes fall in line. Only a handful are unwilling to trade a little self-denial for heaven.

But Jesus isn't finished. "If anyone would come after me, he must deny himself *and take up his cross daily and follow me*." When he spoke those words in the days of his ministry, most, if not all, of his disciples had no idea what he meant. Now, however, as Jesus trudges toward his execution and they hide behind corners and in dark doorways, as they pull their turbans down to shadow their eyes and disguise their faces – now, as they see their master beaten, bleeding, struggling under his cross – NOW they understand!

"No! Is *that* what he meant when he told us to take up our cross daily and follow him?" they ask, trembling.

To be honest, even after meditating on his Passion, I wonder if any of us have the faintest idea of what Jesus meant when he spoke of taking up our cross and following him. At the first step on the way, when we see Jesus condemned to death, we're humbled by our lack of authority to judge anyone. Now, we are humbled even further as we see Jesus, in his innocence, carrying his own cross – showing us how to carry ours.

Only now, as Jesus carries his cross, do the disciples finally see that Jesus was calling them *to consider themselves as good as dead*. They thought they knew what it meant to "take up your cross." But here on a hot, dusty street in Jerusalem, watching the Master take one painful step after another, carrying that cross toward his death, they at last *can see* what he was talking about.

This isn't inspirational visualization, motivational rhetoric or idealistic daydreaming. This isn't Hollywood with its special effects. This is reality. The sweat smells like sweat. The cross is solid wood. The blood is red and real. To "take up your cross" means to struggle ahead toward your own death, struggle against all odds, in whatever manner God calls you to. It means to know you will die . . . to be ready and willing to die as Jesus is now, here on the Via Dolorosa. Just as he *always was ready*.

A Hidden Life

But for the disciples, and for you and me, there is yet another meaning in this scene as Jesus slowly passes by. Jesus moves toward his own physical death, and we must be ready to lose our own physical lives for him, as Paul was. The great apostle said, "As it is written: 'For your sake we face death all day long; we are considered as sheep to be slaughtered'" (Romans 8:36). But it may be just as difficult, or even more difficult, to crucify ourselves *spiritually*. Paul also said, "For if you live according to the sinful nature, you will die; but if by the Spirit you put to death the misdeeds of the body, you will live . . ." (Romans 8:13).

That's tough! Because we love our misdeeds. That is to say, we love our pride, our worldly habits, our human desires.

The Colossian Christians were told, "Set your minds on things above, not on earthly things. For you died, and your life is now hidden with Christ in God . . . . Put to death, therefore, whatever belongs to your earthly nature . . ." (Colossians 3:2-5). The true cross isn't an ornament to wear, it's an instrument upon which to *kill someone*. Many people in this world, even those with no faith at all, adorn themselves with crosses. But the discerning disciple knows that he takes up his cross daily, not as a clothing accessory, but as a means of crucifixion. Crosses are for killing people.

When we come to Christ, our old sinful, natural

person is put to death. God promises that, in baptism, somehow we identify with the death of Jesus – and we also identify with his resurrection (Romans 6). But the desires of the old sinful, natural self tend to resurface. That's when we must put our evil nature to death again, as the Colossians were instructed.

Most of us know that, even though it's the spiritual self rather than the physical self we're dealing with, it's far from painless. Any recovering alcoholic or drug abuser knows that it's easier to end the physical life in a split second than to struggle painfully on, day by day, against powerful inner compulsions. But that's how spiritual victories are won – step by step, toward Calvary.

"If you want to be one of my people," Jesus is saying, "you've got to deny yourself." An honest look at contemporary Christians reveals that many of us seem to be kidding ourselves much of the time. Certainly, there are thousands of disciples who live sacrificially – giving their hearts, their time, their strength and their money to the Lord. But many more thousands of us don't really deny ourselves much of anything. To the contrary, we *exalt ourselves*! Everywhere, every day – we seem to be consumed by self-interest.

When we truly deny ourselves, we'll live more modest lives. There will be less opulence in the homes and church buildings we build, fewer unnecessary possessions and more relief for the suffering people of the world. When we deny ourselves, there will be less narcissism in our church fellowships and more selflessness in our relationships. When we deny ourselves, Jesus will walk the world again, touching and healing through us.

As we see our teacher carrying his cross, perhaps we can hear the challenge of Dietrich Bonhoeffer from a World War II German concentration camp: "When Christ calls a man, he bids him come and die." That "dying" is a *death to self*, and it means separating ourselves from our selfish desires. It means considering ourselves as good as dead – yet very much alive in Christ . . . more alive than any other people on earth.

Three of the desires that plague us most are the desire for wealth, the desire for power and the desire for prestige or popularity. I may not have a desire to live as a millionaire or to be a world leader or a movie star. But I still love comfort and fine things far too much; I crave approval and praise; and I confess that I try to win and exert power over others at times. So, *daily* I must remind myself that I'm a dead man.

When it comes to cross-bearing, God will help us carry whatever burden he lays on us. It may be the loss of loved ones or the loss of our possessions or the loss of reputation. Or it may be something as mundane as having to work in a difficult job or endure monotony. Whatever we carry, we can bear it . . . as if it were the cross of Jesus.

Again it's time to move on in our journey. Before we leave our place of reflection, however, look again at the man with the cross. The Carpenter labors with his wood once more. He labors not with hammer or chisel, but with hand and shoulder and heart. He lifts, pushes forward, staggers, slumps, halts momentarily. Then he repeats the painful process – again and again. He carries his cross.

We, too, are carpenters laboring with wood. We, too, must bear our own crosses if we are faithful to our Master. But the cross each of us bears has nothing to do with taking away sin. Only the Lord Jesus does that, and only he has earned the right to sit with the Father in heaven.

Yet here he is, God in human form, prodded along by the soldiers like some lowly beast of burden. Dirty, bleeding, soon to die . . . he labors with wood.

Chapter Three

LEARNING TO STAND AGAIN

"Oh, lift me as a wave, a leaf, a cloud!
I fall upon the thorns of life! I bleed!"

– Percy Bysshe Shelley, 1819
Ode to the West Wind

There is not a specific passage in the New Testament that tells us that Jesus falls under the weight of the cross as he carries it through the streets of Jerusalem. But it's a reasonable conclusion as we consider his weakened condition and as we read about the bystander who is compelled to carry the cross at one point.

Jesus falling along the way of sorrows is a terribly sad thing to think about. However, from a different perspective, it is incredibly encouraging. But before we meditate upon these thoughts, let's glance back over the past several hours in order to appreciate this scene more fully.

The Night Before

About twelve hours ago, Jesus and his friends shared a final meal together, a supper that was very much like the Passover. The Son of Man knew what lay before him. He knew – and told the disciples – that he wouldn't eat the Passover again until he ate it anew with them in the kingdom that was coming.

It was a beautiful supper, with rich new meaning added to the traditional Hebrew fellowship meal of remembrance. But there were also tense moments as well, because Jesus was aware of the plot that was under way to end his life. He knew that one of his own personally-chosen apostles was a traitor. In fact, the shameful betrayal contract was consummated *during the farewell meal* after Jesus dismissed Judas to "do what he must do," while the rest of the apostles finished their precious last supper.

The stress of betrayal was heart-rending. But the long hours that followed were infinitely more torturous to Jesus' soul. After they had sung a hymn together, they walked out of the city, across the Kidron Valley and up onto the Mount of Olives. By the time they reached the middle of the grove where the olive press stood, night had settled over the hill. They could see the warm lights of Jerusalem being lit across the valley. There, directly in their line of sight, was the holy mount and the temple – the symbol of a people, of a religion, of a God. And behind the temple, beyond the city wall and hidden from view, was a second hill – the one on which Jesus would soon die.

Jesus' countenance already was changing dramatically. Throughout supper he had been moved by a marvelous compassion and warmth, even though there had been a note of finality in his voice. After Judas left, Jesus had seemed ambivalent, with a certain resignation mixed with apprehension. Now, in the garden of the olive press, he was engulfed by sadness and foreboding.

He left the disciples and walked on up the hill to pray alone. Hour after hour, he agonized in prayer with his Father in Heaven; deep into the night he struggled with the horror that he knew was imminent. He probably always knew he would be called upon to die, but now the moment had arrived . . . Satan was in the city, in the midst of the conspiracy, determined to do his worst.

Many men have died valiantly in countless battles through the centuries. They've died for noble causes and for ignoble ones, yet they have given themselves freely. Why, then, did Jesus struggle so? Why did he agonize, while others sacrificed their lives without hesitation?

Someday we'll know for certain, but for now we can only speculate. There are at least three possible reasons for his monumental struggle with the approaching crucifixion that come to mind.

First, only he and the Father knew the full extent of what was coming. Only they could see the evil, the violence, the horrible crimes that people are capable of, falling on the head of Jesus. They could see what *all the sin of humanity* looked like – and felt like – as the massive burden descended on Jesus.

What did Jesus see that night in Gethsemane? Did he have a vision of countless sins pressing in on him – tortures, murders, rapes, betrayals, vicious lies, slander, greed? Did he visualize shattered families, molested children – genocides and infanticides? Did he see the horrors of war? The millions of unborn children aborted with silent screams? The faces of the most evil men and women who ever lived? And the most horrible thoughts of even the most ordinary of us?

Did Jesus visualize your disobedience and my disobedience – that which we hoped no one would ever see? And after seeing all this, did he, the sinless One, finally grasp what it would mean to become *guilty* of those multiplied billions of sins?

A second reason that Jesus agonized so terribly may have had something to do with his dual nature. He was God in his basic nature, yet he was a very real man as well. So there may have been a struggle between the immortal and the mortal. The God-nature in Jesus was being called upon to experience *death*. Yet how can that be? God is, by nature, eternal . . . deathless.

Many people believe that there's nothing God can't do and nothing he doesn't know. However, Scripture doesn't really support that idea. The Bible says that God *cannot* lie. In fact, God cannot violate his own nature in many ways – for example, he is faithful and just, therefore, he *cannot* be unfaithful and unjust.

There, in the garden on that fateful night, Jesus may have struggled with the meaning of death in much the way we do, even though he was God Incarnate. The great difference was that he had existed before his birth into human form. God the Word, or Logos-God, existed long before he became Jesus of Nazareth. If you and I, in our humanity, struggle with the reality of death, how much more did he, in his deity, struggle with the concept of mortality?

A third reason Jesus agonized so greatly may have been the thought – or terror – of being separated from God the Father. Jesus said that he and the Father were one (John 17). Father-God and Son-God . . . two personalities of the same Godhead. And now, because of the sins of humanity, the Godhead will be torn apart. It's such a traumatic event that Jesus will later cry out, "My God, my God, why have you forsaken me?"

Whatever the reason or reasons, Jesus struggled in prayer till perspiration fell to the ground as heavy drops of blood. But by the time he looked out into the darkness and saw the line of torches winding its way toward him like a fiery serpent, the worst was over in some ways. The kiss of betrayal, the mock justice, the beatings . . . all the rest would come. But his peace had returned, at least for the moment. And in his soul he knew victory was assured even though great physical suffering remained to be endured.

Jesus had prayed and agonized so deeply that his clothes were drenched in perspiration. Emotionally, he was spent. Then the guards came rushing into the quiet garden with the clanging and banging of armor. The traitor stepped forward and identified his former master with a kiss. The physical ordeal had begun . . . from interrogation to trial to beating post and back again. Finally, he shouldered the cross.

Is it any wonder that, after a sleepless night (perhaps he hadn't slept well in several nights) and after the long ordeal of emotional, spiritual and physical suffering . . . Jesus falls?

His body has been tortured, battered, abused. Now it is failing him. Just as yours and mine fail us at times. For Jesus isn't God dressed up like a man. He is a real man. He bleeds real blood. He shares the weaknesses and limitations of the flesh with you and me. He falls . . . . *JESUS IS ONE OF US!*

When he went away to pray and returned to find the disciples sleeping, he said, "Could you men not keep watch with me for one hour?" Then he added, ". . . The spirit is willing, but the body is weak" (Matthew 26:40,41). He understood how our bodies are subject to fatigue as well as pain. He knew his own body would fail him, even as the disciples' bodies failed them in the garden.

He Identifies With Us!

What is spinning through the Lord's mind as he pushes and drags the cross through the streets of Jerusalem? As the heaviness of the burden buckles his knees and he falls, what thoughts burn in his brain? I believe it isn't only the weight of the heavy cross that causes him to fall, as great as that is. It is also the sickening weight of the sin that God is laying on him. Jesus falls under the burden of sin . . . physically, spiritually and emotionally.

Push your way through the crowd. Look between two spectators and see him there. His knees are raw and scraped bloody by the paving stones on the street as he tries to pull himself up again. He falls . . . under the burden of the heavy wooden beam . . . under the burden of sins – yours, mine, *all the sins* of all time. He falls. In the humanity he shares with us, he falls.

If we've been able to contain ourselves until now, this is the moment we want to rush forward and lift the cross from the fallen Son of Man. He's utterly fatigued, in a way perhaps we've been. He's bleeding, as we have bled. And he falls, as we have fallen. It's at this place along the way that we really identify with Jesus the man. We may not have agonized in prayer all night long. We may not have been arrested, convicted, sentenced. We may not have been beaten, persecuted and compelled to carry the instrument of our execution. But, at one time or another, we've all fallen; we've been bruised, been scratched, been cut – physically and emotionally. It's a very visible indication of the vulnerability of our humanity, one that may embarrass or humiliate us at times. Yes, we've all fallen. Because we are human.

As Jesus falls, we see how *completely* he identifies with us. The One who falls under his horrible burden will not look away when you and I fall under ours. When we are down and nearly out, he's there at our side. He won't leave us and allow us to fall alone, as a panicked sightless person in an unfriendly and unfamiliar place. He understands the physical difficulties of life – the disabilities, the illnesses, the weaknesses of the flesh. And he also understands our spiritual and emotional difficulties as well. When sin or problems lay heavy on our shoulders and we fall, he's there . . . at our side to lift the burden.

In fact, it was the One who fell under the burden of his cross who said, "Come to me, all you who are weary and burdened, and I will give you rest. Take my yoke upon you and learn from me, for I am gentle and humble in heart, and you will find rest for your souls. For my yoke is easy and my burden is light" (Matthew 11:28-30).

How can he say that his "yoke is easy" and his "burden is light"? The picture before us now is a frightful one. We see a man laboring under a torturous burden, under a yoke of death.

The answer is, the yoke and the burden he's carrying to the cross *are not his own*. They're ours. He's carrying *our* burden, *our* sin; he falls under *our* yoke of condemnation.

On the other hand, his own yoke and burden are to love and serve God and to love and serve humanity. That's what he offers to us. We take on his mission to love and serve . . . he takes on our transgressions – he falls and finally dies under the penalty of our sin.

Most of us are aware that Jesus "has been tempted in every way, just as we are – yet was without sin" (Hebrews 4:15). Perhaps like you, I usually focus on the part that says, "yet was without sin." It's difficult to imagine one who could be tempted like I am, yet be strong enough to succeed where I've failed. However, the writer of Hebrews wasn't trying to discourage us. The first part of that passage says, "For we do not have a high priest who is *unable to sympathize* with our weaknesses . . . ."

Am I alone in feeling at times that Jesus IS unable to sympathize with my weaknesses? Have you ever felt that Jesus' strength makes it difficult for him to understand your frailties?

In our competitiveness, we often think of the winner as one who, openly or secretly, gloats over his or her victory. But when Jesus "won" in his battle against temptation, he didn't gloat – he *sympathized* with our weaknesses. He understood, he understands how difficult it is for us to overcome pride and overcome the strong desires of the flesh.

Here, on the way of the cross, Jesus falls as we all do. He is subject to the same physical human weaknesses that we are. He chooses not to escape from the ordeal, from the pain and anguish, but to endure it. It is good to continually remind ourselves that Jesus' earthly body was just like ours, with nerve endings that send excruciating signals to the brain and central nervous system just as ours do. He isn't a Superman with superhuman strength and invincibility, nor is he some kind of ghost, without substance or physical sensitivities.

He falls as we all do. And he will not ignore our pain and weakness, nor the illnesses that ravage us. He knows. He cares.

God in Human Weakness

The Omnipotent God who created the vast universe has become a man who, at this moment, is too weak to carry a wooden cross – too weak to even stand. That is a concept that we need to get firmly in mind. Because it is at the heart of the reality of the Incarnation! God in human form is also God in human weakness. Perhaps if we can begin to grasp the extent of Jesus' identification with us, we'll reach out to identify with him.

Perhaps if we understand that Jesus persevered and was patient with his weaknesses, we can accept our own human frailties without complaining. What is it that you don't like about yourself? Do you have "defects" in your body – your appearance, some illness, a disability? Do you have a "personality problem" – shy, impetuous, abrasive? If you are less than "beautiful," if you lack social graces, if you are weak, tired, irritated, despondent, depressed – if you feel like a failure – Jesus says to you, "I understand your weaknesses, whether real or only imagined. There was a time when I couldn't even stand upright like a man."

Jesus descended from the realm of perfection to the realm of imperfection. From the strength of heaven to the weakness of earth. That's a long, long journey downward! Surely we can deal with our failures and frailties without becoming paralyzed by despair.

Christians fall. And Jesus falls, too. Of course, when Jesus falls as a result of the weakness in his body, it is not the same as sin. Even though his body is weakened, his character never wavers. Unfortunately, we have weaknesses in both body and character; we fall physically and spiritually. That's the gulf between Jesus and us: the great character gap.

Even though we can't put our full confidence in people because of their limitations, we can, nevertheless, be tolerant toward their failures. Sometimes we are shocked when a Christian mentor or friend doesn't measure up to the stature of his or her convictions. But the truth is, we fall too, and we disappoint our God and our fellow Christians just as others do. That is not to say that we should excuse sin – we must condemn it while we encourage the one who has sinned.

Jesus reveals his weakness to us in a visible way. He identifies with our humanity. And when we see humanity in those around us – or in ourselves – perhaps we can remember to be patient and understanding. The apostle John said, "If we claim to be without sin, we deceive ourselves and the truth is not in us" (1 John 1:8). We have a right to expect improvement in ourselves and in others, but we can't expect to be without sin. So, weakness shouldn't surprise us.

Jesus falls. But he also struggles to his feet again. And that is an encouraging lesson at this step on the way to glory. Like Jesus, we will fall . . . but also like Jesus, we can struggle to our feet through his power.

Because he falls, we can rise . . . he will lift us up.

He'll reach down to us when our knees are bloody and weak. Because he identifies with us – even in our sin and powerlessness.

Our third reflection on the way of the cross is a call to develop patience with our own weaknesses and, especially, with the weaknesses of others. It is a summons to learn to persevere. We can expect to fall – but we must *decide to stand again* and move toward glory.

He Understands

Listen with me as a gasp rolls through the crowd lining the street. "The Lord is falling," sob the women who love and serve him. They surge forward but are repelled by the soldiers who cordon off the area with the shafts of their spears.

His legs shake as he wills himself to stand. He's up again, and the soldiers yell at him to move along. A few moments more and the procession has passed. Some of the crowd join in the cruel parade . . . the rest drift back to their lives wondering about the man on the way to the cross, the man who fell . . . .

But we stand motionless, staring at the place where it happened. The clanging of the death squad, the beating of the drum and the babbling of the throng drift down the street. An eerie silence is left behind, punctuated only by the barking of a dog somewhere and the occasional chirping of a bird.

We walk over to the exact spot where it happened. There are small smudges of blood on two or three of the paving stones. It's his blood.

In a matter of seconds, the blood will be dry. This time tomorrow, the shuffling of sandals along the street will have worn it away, and it will be gone. But we won't forget that he fell. We won't forget the place, the blood that was on the stone. We won't forget.

Life on the street struggles to get back to normal. But

there may be at least a few in the neighborhood who suspect that things will never be quite the same. For there's more to this event than we can comprehend.

Jesus understands when we fall. He didn't come to condemn us; he came so that we can rise up when we fall. Because he understands about falling.

Chapter Four

A VESSEL FOR GOD'S USE

"Who ran to help me when I fell,
And would some pretty story tell,
Or kiss the place to make it well?
My mother."

– Ann Taylor, 1804
Original Poems for Infant Minds

Tradition tells us that there was a brief meeting between Jesus and his mother, Mary, on the way to the cross. Although the New Testament doesn't recount such a meeting, it certainly wouldn't have been unlikely or impossible for such a meeting to take place. In fact, I believe Mary was indeed there . . . there on the way to the Place of the Skull.

Matthew tells us, "Many women were there [at the cross], watching from a distance. They had followed Jesus from Galilee to care for his needs" (Matthew 27:55). Of course, we know from John's record that Mary was there. "Near the cross of Jesus stood his mother, his mother's sister, Mary the wife of Clopas, and Mary Magdalene. When Jesus saw his mother there, and the disciple whom he loved standing nearby, he said to his mother, 'Dear woman, here is your son,' and to the disciple, 'Here is your mother.' From that time on, this disciple took her into his home" (John 19:25-27).

I believe that Jesus met his mother along the way, somewhere on the streets between the Fortress Antonia and Golgotha. Perhaps she and the other women were outside the gate of Pontius Pilate's garrison at daybreak when the news spread that Jesus had been arrested during the night. Perhaps one of the disciples ran from the garden of Gethsemane, awakened the women and told them of the arrest. It seems inconceivable that such serious news wouldn't be communicated to Mary immediately and that she wouldn't be there to offer her love and support.

No doubt the women stood far out on the edge of the blood-thirsty mob, shocked, dismayed that the people could hate this One whom they loved so much. And as the death squad opened the gate and moved their prisoner into the street, the women probably followed at the rear of the procession.

It's likely that Mary would have followed the grim proceedings as they developed, rather than simply going directly to the place of execution and waiting for the death squad to arrive – if she knew where that place was.

Yes, I'm almost sure she was in the crowd, and I believe there was at least one fleeting moment when she moved through the jumble of curious spectators and approached her beloved son. I can almost see it . . .

A Mother and Her Son

There is a slight pressure on our arms, and as we turn to identify the source, a woman slips between us, stepping directly into the street. We see her face for only a split second – yet it is etched in our memory. Her eyes are filled with pain, her cheeks are flushed and streaked by tears, her brow is knit in sadness . . . she is oblivious to us and to all but the center of her gaze.

She's ordinary looking enough to disappear in a crowd. Still, if you stop and really focus on her, as you might in a conversation, she is a striking woman indeed.

She is small and somewhere near fifty, but could pass for a younger woman. However, that isn't what makes her striking. It is her eyes. They are like deep pools of clear water, like crystal springs. You feel as though you can look into her eyes and see her soul. And the soul that's visible there in the depths is a truly remarkable one.

She steps into the street and straight up to the first condemned man, who has paused for a moment to catch his heaving breath. Is it the slightness of her person that causes her to go unnoticed for a minute? Or is it the unexpected audacity?

The prisoner's head rests on his chest, but he sees a small, familiar shadow cross his path. With the back of his hand, he wipes the salty sweat and blood from his eyes, then looks up. For the first time, we see *his eyes*! They are the same deep, clear pools as the woman's . . . they are her eyes!

As the gazes of mother and son meet, in an instant, lengthy conversations seem to pass between them . . . without a word being spoken. Her small hand brushes the blood-stiffened hair from his eyes, as if he were a little boy again, returning home from playful summer fields. The touch of her fingertips on his forehead is like a cool, invigorating breeze. The faint hint of a smile flits across his cracked lips – then is gone.

The moment is shattered as a large, battle-hardened soldier steps up and raises his spear shaft. The woman glances up with eyebrows pressed together in grief. The Roman lowers the spear slowly and simply pulls gently on her shoulder. A last time, her eyes bathe his face in an invisible ointment of love. Then she retreats a pace or two as the procession picks up the cadence of the death drum again and is on its solemn way.

There is a look of horror and helplessness on Mary's face as Jesus lifts and pushes his cross ahead. As only mothers can, she feels every ache and pain that her son experiences. Her heart is breaking, but she must be brave, she must have faith . . . just as he admonished her.

There's no stopping the new tears that well up, then spill over the pools of her eyes. The grim scene before her is blurred by the flood, and suddenly her mind is flying back over the years, to images from other, better times – the strapping young carpenter in whom she took such pride, the 12-year-old boy she found asking and answering profound questions with the temple scholars, the beautiful infant at her breast, rocked to sleep by the swaying of the donkey on the way to Egypt. It was only yesterday, wasn't it? . . .

Specially Chosen by God

Many biblical scholars believe that Mary was still a teenager when she was engaged to Joseph, who was probably a much older man. They lived in the little town of Nazareth, in the central hill country of lower Galilee, north of Jerusalem.

I find it intriguing – and rather remarkable – that three of the four gospel writers don't record the visitation of Mary by a heavenly messenger. In fact, both Mark and John begin their accounts of Jesus with his forerunner John the baptizer, completely overlooking the story of Mary, Joseph and the birth of Jesus. Matthew does record the birth but focuses more on Joseph than on Mary, telling of the dreams when God spoke to Joseph about his bride-to-be, about the child and about safety from those who sought to kill the child.

Luke alone tells future generations of the humble young woman who was specially chosen by God to bear his only son. Is it merely a coincidence that the other three writers are Jewish and Luke is a Gentile? Perhaps. But the Jewish culture was so biased toward men that it's not surprising that Matthew, Mark and John don't bother to mention that *it was a woman* who first was told the specifics of God's plan to redeem humanity. Did the gospel writers not *know* about the visitation of Mary? Or did they simply choose not to record it? One thing is certain: many generations have been thankful that Luke carefully investigated all the stories (Luke 1:3) and was guided by the Holy Spirit to include God's message to Mary – and Mary's thrilling "Magnificat."

The first mention of the mother of Jesus was not by name but by status – and as the object of a mission by a high ranking angel. "In the sixth month [of Elizabeth's pregnancy], God sent the angel Gabriel to Nazareth, a town in Galilee, to a virgin pledged to be married to a man named Joseph, a descendant of David." Then Luke adds, "The virgin's name was Mary" (Luke 1:26,27).

What's the significance of this visit and of the words of the angel? They are earth-shaking! For, the same heavenly messenger, Gabriel, had been sent to Jerusalem six months earlier with the news of the coming birth of John, who would be called "the baptizer." And on that occasion, whom did Gabriel visit? Gabriel appeared in front of the curtain of the holiest place on earth, standing next to the altar of incense inside the temple of God – and spoke to the priest Zechariah. He told Zechariah – a man – that his wife, Elizabeth, would have a child in her old age. The Jews of that day would certainly think, "Yes, that's the way it should be. God doesn't speak to women. If he wants a woman to know that she is miraculously with child, he will tell her husband."

In his gospel, Matthew tells of the dream that Joseph had when the angel said, ". . . do not be afraid to take Mary home as your wife, because what is conceived in her is from the Holy Spirit" (Matthew 1:20). But of course, that dream and that message came after a much more *profound visitation* – a visitation Matthew doesn't record for some reason.

God had told the Israelites centuries ago that he would meet them in the tabernacle and, later, in the temple. God himself said he would dwell in the Holy of Holies. Now the angel Gabriel, whose usual place is in the presence of Almighty God, stands in front of the Holy of Holies – again in the presence of God – and reveals God's will to Zechariah. A few months later, he appears to Mary – and I would suggest that once again, he is standing in the presence of God. God is there in Mary's room, and he is setting the stage for the most astonishing event in human history: the Incarnation of the second person of the Godhead.

Listen to Gabriel's words to Mary, as recorded by Luke: "Greetings, you who are highly favored! The Lord is with you" (Luke 1:28). There's no message in scripture quite like that one. And it was spoken, not to Zechariah or Joseph or any other man, but to a humble little Jewish maiden.

An Angel Comes Calling

No doubt Mary was still living in her parents' home when this momentous event took place. I envision her in a room alone; perhaps she is sewing or weaving. She catches a movement out of the corner of her eye and looks up. There, in the room before her, stands a man . . . "y-yes, a man and not my imagination," she assures herself, trembling as she recovers from the start. "But there's something different about him," she is thinking, "something unearthly. How did he enter the room without me seeing or hearing him? Why did he come uninvited?"

It's then, as the questions rush in on her, that he speaks. The voice is gentle and human, but with a strange, unidentifiable quality.

"Greetings, you who are highly favored!"

Her eyes dart side to side. "Who's he speaking to?"

she thinks. "There's no one nearby. Surely he isn't talking to me!"

The man continues. "The Lord is with you."

Now the full impact of the encounter strikes Mary. "This is *an angel of the Lord*! Right here in my home . . . talking to me!"

Her excitement turns to fear. "But who am I that an angel should visit me?" she thinks. "What does he want with me? I'm a nobody. Why would a messenger of God greet me, saying, 'You are highly favored'?"

Gabriel seems to know her thoughts and says, "Do not be afraid, Mary, you have found favor with God. You will be with child and give birth to a son, and you are to give him the name Jesus. He will be great and will be called the Son of the Most High. The Lord God will give him the throne of his father David, and he will reign over the house of Jacob forever; his kingdom will never end" (Luke 1:30-33).

Her thoughts race. ". . . favor with God . . . with child . . . give birth . . . the name Jesus . . . called the Son of the Most High . . . will reign forever . . . ."

Then she returns to the starting point. She frowns in puzzlement and asks the angel, "How will this be, since I am a virgin?"

He answers, "The Holy Spirit will come upon you, and the power of the Most High will overshadow you. So the holy one to be born will be called the Son of God. Even Elizabeth your relative is going to have a child in her old age, and she who was said to be barren is in her sixth month. For nothing is impossible with God" (Luke 1:35-37).

By this time, Mary is on her knees. Bending low, she whispers, "I am the Lord's servant. May it be to me as you have said." When she looks up, the angel is gone. But the room is filled with glory, with a feeling of power that few humans have experienced.

The Magnificat

The humility and trust that are evident in her submissive statement are amazing. Later, as she travels to the hill country of Judea to visit Elizabeth, Mary breaks into a song of incredible beauty. It is often called the *Magnificat* (after the first word of the Latin text):

> My soul glorifies the Lord and my spirit rejoices in God my Savior, for he has been mindful of the humble state of his servant. From now on all generations will call me blessed, for the Mighty One has done great things for me – holy is his name (Luke 1:46-49).

Her words continue to gracefully flow on as she spontaneously composes phrase after beautiful phrase. And it somehow lifts the soul to read them over and over again, as her hymn of praise recounts God's faithfulness, justice, power and concern for the humble.

She was right in her prophetic statement – all generations *have* called her blessed. The chosen vessel of God, through whom the human form of God was born, is blessed forever! What a singular honor was bestowed upon Mary! What an amazing honor was bestowed upon *all women* through her. For, it was a woman (Eve) who first reached out to take the forbidden fruit in that primordial Garden. Now a woman (Mary) is chosen by God to be the conduit of forgiveness for that sin – and every sin since that time. Through her body, through child-bearing, comes the Savior of all mankind. Truly, Mary was blessed, and is blessed forever; and we are blessed because of her.

I'm astounded as I consider that God, through his Spirit, actually entered a human body and planted his own seed there. It's staggering to think that the Incarnate God grew inside a human being. I don't believe God wants us to worship Mary or reverence her in a way that is reserved for God alone, but neither do I believe God wants us to ignore her. The angel said that Mary was "highly favored," that the Lord was with her, that she had "found favor with God." She prophesied that, "from now on all generations will call [her] blessed, for the Mighty One has done great things for [her] . . . ." And so she must take her place with the greatest who ever lived.

Christ in You

But if it's astonishing to consider the Holy Spirit coming upon Mary and the power of the Most High overshadowing her, think of this: Paul said, ". . . I am again in the pains of childbirth until Christ is formed in you . . ." (Galatians 4:19). And again, "But if Christ is in you, your body is dead because of sin, yet your spirit is alive because of righteousness. And if the Spirit of him who raised Jesus from the dead is living in you, he who raised Christ from the dead will also give life to your mortal bodies through his Spirit who lives in you" (Romans 8:10,11).

Christ was physically formed within Mary. But he is spiritually formed within us – that is, through the Holy Spirit, Jesus becomes real within us! He is in us as surely as he was in Mary, for spiritual realities are no less sure than physical realities. The Colossians were told that God has chosen to make known the glorious riches of the mystery that had been kept hidden for ages, "which is Christ in you, the hope of glory" (Colossians 1:27).

Mary is our ultimate example of Christian servanthood. Others pushed the frontiers of the faith to the uttermost corners of the earth. Others preached the gospel of Christ and gave their lives for the cross of Christ. But only one person said, "I am the Lord's servant. May it be to me as you have said" – whereupon God, through his Spirit, entered her body and planted the seed of the Son of God. Deity literally grew inside her. May God grow spiritually in *our* inmost parts also!

A Bond of Truth

On the way of the cross, their eyes meet in the midst of tremendous tragedy. For a moment, she is mother again of a beautiful, tiny infant in the corner of a stable, with the pungent smell of hay and animals all around.

The eyes she sees now are narrow with pain, lined with agony, but somehow they are the same soft eyes of the baby she clutched long ago. They are still filled with eternity.

Love surges between them like a river. The death squad moves on down the street, and she reaches out into the increasing space between them, as if to say, "O my son, how I wish I could relieve your sorrows; how I wish I could take your pain myself." And I honestly believe that Mary would have died in his place if she could. Just as most mothers would.

He lifts a weak hand, as if to say, "Yes, Mother, I know. You bore me in pain those many years ago; you gave yourself to my Father in heaven to be his holy vessel. Then you gave your young womanhood to raising me to manhood. But this present pain, this present death, I must bear alone. Because it is for you, dear woman, as well as for the whole world that I die. It is for you . . . ."

Of all people who have lived on this earth, only one knew for sure exactly how Jesus was conceived. There are many people, even theologians, who cannot believe in the virgin birth of Jesus. They call into question the testimony of God's word. In effect, they say to Mary, "You were mistaken or deceived. There was no angel. There was no Holy Spirit. There was just an illegitimate child."

But Mary, the blessed one, knows better – she alone

knows the truth for certain. And we will call her blessed forever!

Of course, Jesus knows the truth, too, but in a different way. It was revealed to him by his Father. The rest of us know the truth by faith.

So, only two people on earth know for certain who Jesus really is – one knows by her experience, the other knows by revelation from his Father. Only two know for certain Jesus' origin from the Holy Spirit. And it is these two, between whom there is this bond of truth, who meet ever so briefly on the way of sorrows.

A few precious seconds, then the soldiers push the condemned men on. But I believe I saw them there together . . . a mother, a son . . . a woman, a Savior. Did you see them, too?

Chapter Five

WALKING IN HIS STEPS

"Yes'm, old friends is always best, 'less you can catch a new one that's fit to make an old one out of."

– Sarah Orne Jewett, 1896
The Country of the Pointed Firs

It is fascinating how two individual lives seem to come from different directions like highways in the desert and finally intersect with profound implications. Sometimes, after only a brief encounter, one or both of the lives are never the same again. That is certainly true of the incident to which we now come on the road to glory.

I envision it happening like this . . .

Self-appointed messengers are running ahead of the Roman soldiers and their Jewish prisoners, alerting the people on the street of the spectacle that's approaching. Faces peer out from darkened windows, from behind partially closed doors. The din of the crowd increases noticeably . . . the anticipation mounts.

Then, like the wake of a ship as it slices through the water, the multitude rolls back against either side of the narrow street. And the death squad slices through. The excited babble of close-pressed voices is suddenly interrupted – a strange silence grips the spectators as they look into the faces of the three men who are about to die.

A Passover Pilgrim in Town

Several weeks earlier in a city far away in North Africa, a Jewish man prepared to leave his home on a long, hot and dangerous journey. The man's name was Simon, and his destination was God's holy city.

The desire of every devout Jew was to "go up to Jerusalem" for that most important, that most ethnic of their celebrations, the Passover. It was the first feast of the Jewish year, and every male was required by Mosaic Law to attend Passover if it was physically possible. And this year, Simon was finally able to make the difficult journey.

Even in our own day, in an air-conditioned automobile, we might be a little hesitant to cross such a large expanse of desolate country – from Libya to Israel – just for a feast. But it wasn't just *any* feast. It was the feast of Passover – a remembrance of that ancient time when God spared the Hebrews from the death angel, "passing over" the homes of the faithful who had marked them with the blood of a lamb. It was the Passover that marked the beginning of the Hebrew people as a distinct nation. The family of Jacob had entered Egypt, the nation of Israel had marched out.

And so Simon set out from Cyrene, an oasis in the desert of what is today Libya. At an elevation of about 2,000 feet above sea level and only 10 miles from the Mediterranean Sea, the city had a delightful climate compared to the searing heat of the Sahara. In addition, the soil was fertile and the location so valuable that the Greeks who settled the city at the turn of the sixth century B.C. planned to make Cyrene the "Athens of Africa."

Simon may have taken a ship and sailed along the

coast to one of the ports of Palestine, but it's more likely that he walked the entire journey to Jerusalem. He would have crossed the Libyan desert, the Nile Delta in Egypt and finally the Gaza strip before entering Judea. And at long last, as he climbed the hill country, he would have looked up and thrilled to see the holy city, with its majestic temple mount, gleaming in the Judean sun. The sight must have quickened his pulse. And he might have said to himself, "My life is in Cyrene, far away, but my soul is here, in this city . . . in this holy temple of God."

Simon had savored the last few hours, visiting with relatives, openly enjoying the traditional Jewish life – and most of all, worshiping in the temple courts. Now he is weaving his way along the streets, through the holiday crowds, doing some last minute shopping and sight-seeing before the Passover. Thousands of others who have made the pilgrimage to Jerusalem are doing the same. There are herbs and wine and bread and lamb to buy. Perhaps even a new robe for such a special occasion.

"How in the world do they pack all these people into the holy city?" he is thinking. "And they are all Jews! Ah, there are so few of my brothers and sisters back in Cyrene. It feels good to be in the majority for a change – even if it is under the watchful eyes of the Romans. I love the sights and sounds and smells of this place!"

His pleasant and contented thoughts are suddenly interrupted by the yelling of men farther up the street. The note of alarm rises above the noise of the holiday throng. Now he can hear the clanging of metal, the snapping of whips, and the rhythmic, ominous beating of a drum moving toward him. He turns and starts to walk away. "The one thing I don't need on a holiday is trouble, and this sounds like trouble!" he says to no one in particular.

But his curiosity is too great. He plants his feet, cranes his neck, and rises to his toes to get a glimpse of the movement in the center of the sea of people.

Simon notices the crowd around him edging sideways, pushed like a wave by an advancing force, until the people are two- or three-deep against each side of the street, pressed against the houses and shops. He, too, is being moved in a shuffling fashion. But to his dismay, he has ended up on the front row on his side of the narrow street.

Louder and louder the frightening martial sounds echo between the ancient cobblestones and walls. Simon's stomach knots up with a sickening feeling – for he can see them plainly now. The soldiers in front carry long spears to press the crowds back. Immediately behind them, two others periodically draw their whips back and, in one fluid motion, snap the woven leather strips forward with a vicious and earsplitting crack.

Simon moves his head from side to side in order to see around the soldiers. He has seen Roman soldiers in his hometown many times – enough to last a lifetime, in fact. But he now has a certain compulsion to see the condemned. Is it his sense of compassion? Simple curiosity? Or is it a feeling of relief that it is someone else and not he who will soon die?

"There! There are the condemned ones, poor wretches," he thinks. "Three of them. I wonder what they have done? What have they done that's worthy of death? Probably nothing, if I know these Roman dogs!"

He Sees Jesus

The ugly procession is now beginning to pass right in front of Simon. The noise of the whips, drum and rattling armor is deafening. He leans close to the man standing near him, cups his mouth with his hand and asks above the din, "Who are they? What are their crimes – does anyone know?"

The man frowns as he throws a quick glance at Simon. "You must be from out of town! The whole city is full of the news. Those last two fellows are thieves – maybe insurrectionists, if you believe the Roman governor. But that first man there . . . he's the teacher from Galilee who's causing the stir. Big crowds have been gathering to hear him preach in the temple courts and out in the countryside. They say he speaks differently than the scribes and Pharisees."

The preacher-prisoner is laboring to carry the wooden instrument upon which he is to die. His physical condition appears to be much worse than the other two condemned men. His robe is spattered with blood, woven thorn branches have been pressed down on his head, his knees are about to buckle.

Simon's neighbor cocks his head closer and whispers, "Look at him. You know it's got to be a trumped up charge. He's a preacher, a rabbi – not a Zealot. Any fool can see that."

Suddenly the prisoner collapses to his knees, and the cross he carries crashes down with a heavy, hollow thud. There is an audible gasp from the crowd, from the men and women alike. The procession stops. The drum falls silent.

Simon leans forward instinctively – almost takes a step toward the prisoner, then decides better. "What's the rabbi's name?" he whispers instead.

"Jesus," replies his neighbor. "His name is Jesus."

At that moment, one of the soldiers turns and unleashes his whip toward the fallen rabbi. In a split second, the coarse leather strips coil over the bruised and raw shoulder of the prisoner with a loud snap. Jesus jerks back, crumples to the paving stones in agony.

"You! You there! Get over here and pick up this cross," shouts the officer in charge. He is looking in

Simon's direction.

Simon glances to his right and left, somehow expecting the centurion's gaze to be directed to those on either side. His immediate thought is, "He certainly can't mean me! I'm just a visitor in town. I shouldn't even be here. And I'm certainly not involved in this local scandal!"

But the officer's eyes do not move off his own eyes. They bore into him like a carpenter's drill. Adrenaline shoots through his body instantly like white hot lava, his stomach churns again with a sick feeling. He wants to turn and run, but he's penned in by the crowd in the narrow street. He can't even slip behind another spectator. There's no place to hide.

"I'm talking to you! Move!" yells the centurion. "Pick up that cross or you'll take his place on it. Let's get on with this thing."

Somehow, Simon's weak knees move him forward to the rabbi. He drops to one knee and lifts the heavy cross from Jesus' back. He hoists the wooden beam up onto his own shoulders, steadying himself to rise.

With the weight removed, Jesus struggles valiantly to his knees. And Simon, not yet on his feet, finally turns and looks into the face of Jesus, no more than two feet away.

"Who Are You?"

The Cyrenean winces as he sees the Nazarene's battered nose, swollen and blackened eyes, and the streaks of blood from the thorns on his brow. Then he looks directly into Jesus' eyes – and for a moment, Simon is lost in time.

The eyes of Jesus, despite his young age, seem old – almost ancient – and terribly tired . . . yet somehow they also are filled with life and promise, like the bright eyes of a little child. They communicate wisdom and goodness. But they also are filled with sorrow. They are, to

Simon, windows into another realm.

His mind races. "Who are you?" he thinks. "*What* are you? A rabbi, a preacher, a prophet? How do you know me? You do, don't you? You know all about me! I can sense it. But that's impossible! I'm from a faraway city. We've never seen one another till now, but . . . ."

A sound like an instant clap of thunder splits the air. Instinctively, Simon jumps. It's so loud and so near that it leaves a loud ringing and throbbing in his offended ears. His heart pounds wildly. The soldier's whip has snapped less than a foot from his head. He jerks and pushes up, stands, adjusts the weight of the cross and turns away from Jesus. But his mind does not turn away. The eternal eyes of the Lord seem to burn images on his retinas.

As he takes his first step, Simon is thinking, "What was that name again? . . . Jesus? Yes, that's it. Jesus. What do you want of me, Jesus? This is none of my affair, you know. Are you trying to drag me to the cross with you? I'm only here to celebrate the Passover. I should have turned and walked away when I heard the commotion in the street. That's what curiosity will do for a person. You're standing in a crowd one minute and the next thing you know, you're involved in the execution of a . . . a what? A criminal? Oh, no. Not a criminal." His thought fades as he sees an ocean of eyes watching him from the sides of the street. He can feel his cheeks burn with embarrassment.

"I just can't believe it. I'm a spectator one minute – and the next thing I know, I'm part of the spectacle," Simon thinks. But then his consciousness of the crowd dissolves as his mind returns to the man who is shuffling a few feet in front of him. "Who are you, Jesus?"

Drinking the Lord's Cup

Barely a week has gone by since a rather strange

interchange took place between Jesus and some of his followers. Jesus was on his way to Jerusalem, and he paused along the journey to tell his followers what was in store for him. He said, "We are going up to Jerusalem, and the Son of Man will be betrayed to the chief priests and the teachers of the law. They will condemn him to death and will turn him over to the Gentiles to be mocked and flogged and crucified. On the third day he will be raised to life!" (Matthew 20:18,19).

It was a plain and pointed prophecy of what would shortly happen. But in spite of this recent explanation concerning the end, the disciples simply were unable to grasp it. In fact, one of the women in the group, the mother of James and John, came to Jesus right after he had told them of his impending death and asked a favor of him.

Imagine it! Jesus has just unburdened himself to his loved ones – he will be mocked, flogged, crucified! – and the response of this fine woman and her two sons (one of whom was called "the disciple whom Jesus loved"), was to ask for favors! Does that strike you as strange? Jesus says, "I'm going to die!" She says, "Okay, but when you have your kingdom, can my boys rule with you?"

Actually, what she said to Jesus was, "Grant that one of these two sons of mine may sit at your right and the other at your left in your kingdom."

"You don't know what you are asking," Jesus said to them. "Can you drink the cup I am going to drink?"

It's obvious that this isn't a case of an overzealous mother sneaking behind her sons' backs and trying to manipulate their future. James and John are standing right there, listening to this maternal politicking! Perhaps they even put her up to it. Perhaps they thought, "Jesus might just listen to a loving mother, whereas he might see right through us and our ambition."

The height of their pride and egotism is expressed in their answer to his question, "Can you drink the cup I am going to drink?" The two men confidently say, "We can."

Then Jesus says to them, "You will indeed drink from my cup, but to sit at my right or left is not for me to grant. These places belong to those for whom they have been prepared by my Father" (Matthew 20:20-23). In the moments that follow, he teaches them the difference between Christian servant-leadership and the authority exercised in the world.

"We can," said James and John. "*We can* drink the cup you are going to drink." Did they hear what he had said only minutes before? . . . "They will condemn me to death, mock me, flog me and crucify me." But where are James and John now – here on the way of the cross? A stranger from Cyrene is carrying the cross. Where are Jesus' closest friends and followers? They've run away, they're hiding.

Sometimes closeness leads to blindness. Those who are near the Lord can lose their perspective, if they are not very careful. And sometimes it's strangers who finally see and believe and reach out to Jesus . . . and even carry his cross. In 1717, Alexander Pope wrote:

> "By foreign hands thy dying eyes were closed,
> By foreign hands thy decent limbs composed,
> By foreign hands thy humble grave adorned,
> By strangers honored, and by strangers mourned!"

But Jesus was right. The "Sons of Thunder" *would indeed* drink of his cup. Not so long after this time, James would become the first of the apostle to die, slain by the sword for his faith. And one day John would be exiled to a barren piece of rock called Patmos to "rot" for his allegiance to the Christ.

In the late 1600s, Thomas Shepherd wrote these words: "Must Jesus bear the cross alone, And all the world go free? No, there's a cross for ev'ry one, And there's a cross for me."

Can we really expect to follow Jesus and experience his joy without also experiencing his pain? Can we drink the cup of blessing without drinking the cup of sorrows?

Long ago, Simon was *compelled* to carry the cross of Jesus. But since that time, the followers of Christ have been willingly accepting his sufferings. What did Paul mean when he wrote, "For just as the sufferings of Christ flow over into our lives, so also through Christ our comfort overflows"? (2 Corinthians 1:5). Did he not mean that we must be prepared to receive the same treatment as our Master and that such treatment is sure to come, sooner or later, if we stand openly for Christ? Paul hastened to say that through Christ our comfort will overflow also. But before the comfort, there must be the overflow of pain and humiliation. We're not above our Master.

Simon's Legacy

There's a fascinating reference in Romans 16:13. In Paul's final words to the Roman Christians, he says, "Greet Rufus, chosen in the Lord, and his mother, who has been a mother to me, too." Obviously, the two who are mentioned by Paul are very special people – one is "chosen in the Lord," and the other is a woman who has been like a mother to the apostle Paul. Who is this Rufus? It's very likely that he's none other than the son of Simon the Cyrenean who carries the cross of Jesus. And Rufus' mother, then, would be Simon's wife.

In his gospel, which many believe was written to the church in Rome, Mark describes Simon in the following way: "A certain man from Cyrene, Simon, the father of Alexander and Rufus, was passing by on his way in from the country, and they forced him to carry the cross" (Mark 15:21). It's significant that Mark identifies Simon, not by his father's name, but by his *sons' names* (remember, for example, the apostle Peter's real name was Simon bar Jonah – or Simon *son of* Jonah). That would certainly indicate that Simon's sons were well known in the Christian community – and especially in the church in Rome, the initial destination of Mark's gospel. So when Paul writes to the Roman Christians, he greets his friends and the most faithful Christians there, and among them is Rufus, "chosen in the Lord."

At the very least, the reference in Mark 15:21 seems to tells us that the sons of Simon of Cyrene were well known Christians. And if the reference in Romans 16:3 is speaking of the same Rufus (Rufus bar Simon, if you will), then we should hold him in very high regard – as one "chosen in the Lord" – and we should honor Simon's wife as one who served as "a mother" to the great apostle Paul.

And all of this – Alexander, Rufus and their mother being prominent Christians – strongly suggests that Simon himself was touched deeply by his encounter with Jesus on the way to the cross . . . and that Simon not only followed Jesus, carrying the Lord's cross on *that* day, but that he followed him all the days of his life.

Or is it purely coincidental that the same gospel that says of Simon, "they . . . put the cross on him and made him *carry it* BEHIND Jesus," is also the gospel that earlier quoted Jesus as saying, "If anyone would *come AFTER me*, he must deny himself and *take up his cross daily and FOLLOW me*" and "anyone who does not *carry his cross and FOLLOW me* cannot be my disciple" (Luke 23:26; 9:23; and 14:27)? There seem to be many reasons to believe that Simon did indeed become a follower of

Jesus – not only by Roman compulsion but by choice and by faith. And through his faithfulness, his wife and his sons, Alexander and Rufus, were led to the Lord.

Celebrating the Real Passover

And so we stand and watch from the crowded street. The stranger from faraway North Africa is pressed into duty by the Roman soldiers – the grim duty of carrying a death cross. As he's pulled from the crowd and shoved forward to the fallen prisoner, we can almost hear him say, "What is happening? I came such a long distance, after saving my money for so many years, to celebrate the holy and wonderful feast of Passover. And I find myself compelled to carry an ugly cross! What irony and insult!"

But it's only later that Simon discovers that the *real irony* is not that a Passover celebrant had been pressed into a ceremony of execution. The irony is that he came expecting to celebrate the ancient Passover and, instead, he *participates* in the greatest Passover in history – the TRUE PASSOVER, the one for which Moses' Passover was but a shadow!

Yes, I believe Simon of Cyrene, the first person to ever take up a cross and follow Jesus, would have liked Thomas Shepherd's words very much:

> Must Jesus bear the cross alone,
> And all the world go free?
> No, there's a cross for ev'ry one,
> And there's a cross for me.
>
> The consecrated cross I'll bear
> Till He shall set me free,
> And then go home my crown to wear,
> For there's a crown for me.
>
> O precious cross! O glorious crown!
> O resurrection day!

Ye angels from the stars, come down
And bear my soul away.

It's time to move to the next place of reflection, the next step in our journey to glory. But before we go, look again at this precious scene. The suffering Savior has a few minutes of relief because a man is forced to carry the cross. Simon plods along behind Jesus, wondering who this man is . . . this man whose eyes and mind and heart have touched him – in so brief a time. But one day soon, Simon will carry his own cross gladly. He will be following Jesus with inexpressible joy.

Do you see only Simon there behind Jesus? Or do you see yourself? There's a sense in which every Christian is there, walking behind the Master . . . on the way of the cross.

Do you see Jesus, relieved of his burden for at least a few moments . . . and as you look closely at the person carrying the cross behind the Savior, do you see your face?

Chapter Six

LISTEN TO THE ALARM

> "No longer mourn for me when I am dead
> Than you shall hear the surly sullen bell
> Give warning to the world that I am fled
> From this vile world, with vilest worms to dwell."
>
> – William Shakespeare, 1609
> *Sonnet 71*

If we listen closely, perhaps we can hear the sounds in the streets of Jerusalem on that certain day long ago . . . the rattle of armor, the scraping of wooden beams along the paving stones, the explosive cracking of the whip, the rude yelling and cursing of the soldiers, the beating of the Roman drum, the murmuring of the crowd.

Now, as Simon of Cyrene is compelled to carry the cross, Jesus is able to walk erect, and he focuses on yet another sound coming from behind him. It's the chilling, mournful sound of wailing women following the procession.

The sound drapes a pall over the people, sends a shiver down the backs of even the most hardened. The wail is that anguished protest to death, that release of grief heard so often at Middle Eastern funerals – but even sadder here because the one for whom these women mourn is not dead, he's still alive . . . trudging before them toward his inevitable death.

What happens next, recorded by Luke in his gospel

(23:27-31), seems very strange, somehow out of place with the rest of the drama . . .

Who's in Charge?

In addition to the crowds pressed against the sides of the street, standing in doorways, leaning out of windows and sitting on roofs, there is a multitude of people walking behind the death squad. Why would all these people take time out of their Passover preparations to march behind soldiers bearing three condemned men to their execution?

Of course, there are the prisoners' relatives and friends who want to support their loved ones to the very end. As always, there are the curious – those gawkers motivated by a strange fascination with death. There also are religious leaders, enemies of Jesus, who want to make sure this preacher they hate is properly eliminated. A certain number of people, no doubt, are inadvertently caught up in the sudden drama – shoppers, local neighborhood residents, passersby. Then there's a large number of disciples – followers of the Nazarene rabbi, Jesus.

Near the front of the somber multitude following the soldiers and prisoners are the women, mingling their cries into a ghostly tapestry of mournful moans – sounds of sorrow for the man of sorrows . . .

Then it happens! Jesus stops suddenly, turns and faces the crowd behind him. The wailing women immediately fall silent, shocked to see Jesus facing them. They are jostled by the rest of the crowd as it comes to a stop. The drum ceases. The babbling of the crowd trails off into silence. And the soldiers are so taken by surprise that they simply stand and watch the prisoner to see what he's up to.

It's as if the pause button is pressed on the video

cassette recorder through which we are watching the strange event. The swirling, ugly scene – the confusion and feeling of hopelessness – *everything* is suddenly frozen in place. All eyes are fastened on this One who is supposed to be the object of contempt or pity, this One who is supposed to be helpless.

Odd, isn't it? This "poor wretch" who seems to be at the mercy (or lack of it) of the death squad is suddenly *in control of the entire situation*. He has everyone's attention.

It makes us want to ask, "Who's in charge here, anyway?" That's certainly what the Roman governor, Pilate, wondered a short while ago. As he stood Jesus in the midst of his garrison, under judgment, he kept saying to himself, "I'm in charge here. Of course I'm in charge here! So why is it that I get the feeling that this Jesus fellow is in charge? Doesn't he know who I am? Doesn't he know I have complete power over him?"

But of course Pilate *didn't* have complete power over Jesus. He had only the power that God gave him – which means he wasn't really "in charge" at all. It is times like these – in the judgment hall or here as he stops the procession – that reveal that the Father, through Jesus, is indeed in charge of every eventuality, every detail, every moment of the way . . . even on the way to the Roman cross.

So, everyone waits to see what Jesus will say, what he will do. Each person is like a deer, frozen in the headlights of an automobile . . . .

The Lord's Warning

The silence finally is broken by his voice, at first low, then mounting to surprising strength and clarity.

"Daughters of Jerusalem, do not weep for me!" he says to the amazement of all who can hear.

Whispers immediately hiss among the mourners. "Is

he talking to *us*?" they ask of one another. "Did he say, 'Don't weep for me'? He must be confused by the pain and fatigue, don't you think? Look at his condition . . . I feel so bad for him."

His voice is even stronger now. "Weep for yourselves and for your children!"

The women look to him and then to one another in dismay. "What? What is he talking about?"

Now Jesus speaks with the authority that has caught the imagination of the multitudes. "For the time will come when you will say, 'Blessed are the barren women, the wombs that never bore and the breasts that never nursed!'"

The women suck in their breath. They're immobilized by shock. Every one of them is painfully aware that barrenness is a woman's greatest curse in their society. Hardly anything is worse.

"How could *we ever say*, 'Blessed are the barren women'? No, Lord, that can't be!" they whisper.

But Jesus continues. ". . . They will say to the mountains, 'Fall on us!' and to the hills, 'Cover us!'" He seems to be quoting the prophet Hosea now (10:8).

Jesus pauses for a moment and searches the faces of the people. Then he concludes with a puzzling statement that will send them all home wondering.

"For if men do these things when the tree is green, what will happen when it is dry?"

He stands motionless as his words resonate up and down the street. And through the minds of the people. And through the years.

Then there's silence again. He slowly turns back in the direction of the cross. Now he's ready to move forward.

The commander blinks as if he's been entranced, then it occurs to him that he's lost control of the situation. He clears his throat and begins barking orders.

"That's enough! Move out! What do you think this is, a public forum? Move, move!"

The prominent prisoner obediently moves forward. The centurion glances around, then looks toward Jesus. Both of them know, down deep, who's in charge. Just as Pilate did. One man is a Roman officer, confident in himself and in the Empire that he represents. The other man holds no office, has no wealth, has no weapons of destruction, no earthly power – and he marches to his death. But both men know who's ultimately in command. And the Roman commander shudders – ever so slightly – as he pushes the whole idea out of his mind. After all, he has some crucifixions to carry out.

The procession slowly moves on down the street, followed by the crowd. But the wailers are marching along silently. Their minds swim with questions and anxiety. The remaining people on the street gradually disperse.

But we're left wondering. Did it ever really happen, or was it, perhaps, a daydream? No, we decide, it was indeed real. So, we meditate on it for awhile.

The Daughters of Jerusalem

First of all, we might think about these women who, a moment ago, were mourning and wailing as they accompanied the procession. Who, exactly, are they? Jesus calls them "Daughters of Jerusalem," and there are a few possibilities as to what he might mean by that. He might be addressing them as representatives of all the women of Jerusalem. Or perhaps he has in mind all of Israel – perhaps they're being addressed as representatives of all the women of God. There also is the possibility that they are disciples of Jesus, or maybe more recent followers from his triumphal entry into Jerusalem just a few days ago. Some have suggested that there was a group of godly women in Jerusalem who made it their ministry to mourn at all crucifixions.

The latter explanation is an interesting one, because there were many deeply religious women in Jerusalem at that time. For example, when Mary and Joseph took the infant Jesus to Jerusalem to present him to the Lord, they were met by Anna, the daughter of Phanuel. Anna was a prophetess, an elderly widow who worshiped night and day in the temple, fasting and praying. When she saw the child, "she gave thanks to God and spoke about the child to all who were looking forward to the redemption of Jerusalem" (Luke 2:36-38).

So perhaps the mourners Jesus addressed were a group of devout women who mourned for all those crucified on a Roman cross. However, one part of the text doesn't seem to fit with that explanation. Luke 23:27 says, "A large number of people followed *him*, including women who mourned and wailed *for him.*" It was for Jesus, specifically, that they mourned and not for all the condemned men equally. These women knew Jesus, and apparently loved him enough to be involved in such a public demonstration.

Then perhaps the mourners were the women who traveled with him and ministered to him. The only problem with that explanation is that the women who were numbered with the disciples of the Lord, who ministered to him, were from Nazareth, Capernaum, Bethany, Magdala, and other places as well as Jerusalem. Yet Jesus addressed them by saying, "Daughters of Jerusalem . . . ."

Perhaps the best explanation is that this group of mourners included Jesus' followers from Galilee and also included more recent followers from Jerusalem, as well as a sprinkling of those holy women who had heard that a rabbi was going to be crucified. And Jesus is using the term "daughters of Jerusalem" in a symbolic way, to address both the actual residents of the city and all the daughters of God.

The Alarm

Whoever the women are, Jesus takes this extraordinary moment to offer a prophecy to them concerning a future portentous time – "weep for yourselves and for your children," he says, "for the time will come . . . ." The words he speaks aren't words of condemnation – but words of compassion and pity.

It's always the plight of humans, it seems, to overlook ultimate reality and to see only the immediate fleeting events. These women see only a tortured and condemned man: they see someone to pity. But Jesus sees the coming conflagration of the holy city, the slaughter of her people, and, indeed, the ultimate destruction of the world: he sees multitudes to pity.

Still, it's strange that Jesus would tell the women not to weep for him. Did he not want to encourage compassion among people? Certainly, it's good to be moved by the pain and suffering of another. But their problem, again, was that they didn't see the reality of the present situation. They saw only an abused, innocent man on his way to his execution.

Could they, should they, have seen more? Jesus, only hours earlier, had told his disciples, "Now is the Son of Man glorified and God is glorified in him. If God is glorified in him, God will glorify the Son in himself, and will glorify him at once. My children, I will be with you only a little longer. You will look for me, and just as I told the Jews, so I tell you now: Where I am going, you cannot come" (John 13:31-33).

Later, he had revealed even more. He said, "Now I am going to him who sent me, yet none of you asks me, 'Where are you going?' Because I have said these things, you are filled with grief. But I tell you the truth: It is for your good that I am going away. Unless I go away, the Counselor will not come to you; but if I go, I will send him to you" (John 16:5-7).

Even now, the disciples and the faithful "daughters of Jerusalem" don't ask him where he's going. They would think that an absurd question. "The Lord is going to his death, of course," they would no doubt say in tears. "He's going to the cross."

Yet Jesus himself would probably say something like, "Yes, there is a cross before me; but I will endure that cross. Because that's not where I'm going, ultimately. *I am going to him who sent me. I am going to my Father*! So do not weep for me; I'm going home. Weep for yourselves and for your children, because you have many sorrows to endure, even as I do now."

Just as we usually do, the crowd looks only on the present scene before them. But Jesus looks beyond the curtain upon which the present is painted; he prophesies about the future, saying, "For the time will come when you [you women who are mourning for me] will say, 'Blessed are the barren women, the wombs that never bore and the breasts that never nursed!" The time will come when disaster descends upon the great and noble city of Jerusalem. And it will come before too long.

When the calamity comes, it will be so terrible that the inhabitants of the holy city will say to the mountains, "Fall on us," and to the hills, "Cover us." Jesus seems to echo the ancient words of the prophet Hosea (10:8), but whereas Hosea was addressing the rebellious northern Hebrew tribes, or "Israel" as they were often called, Jesus now applies the warning to the people of the city of God, the capital of Judah. Now *they* are the rebellious ones, and they too will be destroyed.

Earlier, as the Lord made his way toward Jerusalem, he lamented over the city. In Luke 13:31-35, Jesus was told to leave the region where he was teaching and healing because King Herod wanted to kill him. But Jesus replied, "Go tell that fox, 'I will drive out demons and heal people today and tomorrow, and on the third day I will reach my goal.' In any case, I must keep going today and tomorrow, and the next day – for surely no prophet can die outside Jerusalem!"

What an indictment against the people!

He knew death awaited him in the city. He knew the history of how God's spokesmen were treated there – and he mourned, not for himself, but for the people and the place that was supposed to be holy unto Jehovah. Jesus cried out, "O Jerusalem, Jerusalem, you who kill the prophets and stone those sent to you, how often I have longed to gather your children together, as a hen gathers her chicks under her wings, but you were not willing! Look, your house is left to you desolate."

Jesus spoke those words just days ago on the way into the city. Now, on the way to the cross, he warns the wailing daughters of Jerusalem, ". . . weep for yourselves and for your children." Desolation is coming – such that you will say, "The women who have no children are *not* cursed, as you suppose . . . they are *blessed*! They will not have to watch their children die."

For the mourning women and others who understand what Jesus is saying, this is a gracious and wonderful warning. They have the chance to flee the city. And in Jesus, they – and we – have the opportunity to be deemed innocent and flee the final judgment. How many will listen and understand, we wonder?

Saved by Faith

Jesus' last statement to the daughters of Jerusalem is puzzling, because it's spoken like a proverb but also is a question set in the language of analogy, calling the listeners to interpret its meaning. He summarizes his warning to the women by saying, "For if men do these things when the tree is green, what will happen when it is dry?"

In the context, it's difficult to imagine that Jesus is

talking about anything other than his own crucifixion and the coming destruction, about which he is warning the women. He begins, ". . . if men do these things . . . ." Standing there in the street only minutes from his execution, it seems certain that he's referring to the very things that are now happening: the judgment, humiliation and crucifixion of the Son of God. And what is this "tree" to which he refers? Perhaps it is Jesus himself – perhaps he's the tree that is green, that is innocent, fruitful, vibrant, full of life. They're abusing and killing what is productive and good.

The tree also might be Israel, God's people, and while Jesus is with them, they (the tree) are "green" – full of life. Jesus made it clear that he IS LIFE. He creates life, he sustains life, and he himself IS life. And so, if "men" (the Gentiles, specifically the Romans) burn the tree when it's green (good, productive and full of life) – if they disgrace and kill the Son of God – what will they do when THE LIFE (Jesus) is gone and the tree is dry? Of course, it is a rhetorical question, the implied answer being: "They will burn dry Israel, they will bring utter ruin on the great city of Jerusalem, and nothing will be the same again."

Jesus spoke the truth. Only 36 years later, Jerusalem was laid bare; the temple was destroyed – never to be rebuilt; the priesthood was lost; and blood flowed like water in the streets. Survivors were scattered to the wind. The Romans swept through the country and capital city destroying everything in sight.

One has to wonder, did those wailing women who followed Jesus perish? . . . or did they take his warning to heart and flee Jerusalem?

When the destruction of Jerusalem and Israel is finally seen in history, the warning of Jesus becomes obvious. But in A.D. 70, when the disaster struck, it was too late to heed the warning. Listening to a warning and heeding it before the catastrophe strikes . . . is FAITH. Even today, we are *saved by faith* when we heed someone's warning, and it is even truer that faith is what saves us in eternity.

A Different Timetable

One last thought. The passage of time undoubtedly tested the faith of even the most faithful. Those who believed and heeded Jesus' warning must have wondered if they had really understood the Lord when 10, 20, 30 years went by without incident. Their children grew up and had children of their own, and still the end didn't come. Half a lifetime passed before the Romans finally came and leveled Jerusalem. The message to us is: Realize that God isn't on our timetable. He may have graciously delayed the end of all things by 1000, 2000 or more years. But his promises are true and will be fulfilled – just when we think he has forgotten them.

What an extraordinary place of reflection this is! Imagine this happening in the present tense . . . how shocked everyone must be – the Romans, the Jewish leaders, the crowds, the wailing women, the disciples – everyone is taken aback as Jesus stops, turns and confronts the people and specifically the daughters of Jerusalem.

Where's his cringing fear of death? Where's his self-pity and bitterness? Where's his hatred for the persecutors? And where's his questioning of God's providential care?

Even on the way to the cross, Jesus is not thinking of his own pain, but of the grave danger that the people of Jerusalem and Israel are in . . . and of the greater danger that hangs over the whole world because of the rebellion of each individual.

This scene that's played out before us demonstrates

that Jesus is still in control – even when he is "like a lamb that is led to slaughter," in the words of the prophet Isaiah. Though by outward indications all is lost, our Lord is shown to be the only one in the multitude who is saved. It is *they who are in peril* . . . and in compassion, he warns the wailing women.

Why did he specifically focus on the women? Their mourning was loud, of course, and must have drawn considerable attention to them. But somehow I believe he spoke to the women, not because their mourning was so noisy and obvious, but because he knew of their faith, their sensitivity, their desire to nurture and build up, their thirst for devotion. These were the "sisters" of Mary, his mother, that precious conduit of God. Some of them would be near the cross, *stay* near the cross, while the male disciples ran and hid as they saw their dream die.

Perhaps in some way, Jesus' warning is a tribute to women. For the last time he tells of the coming destruction . . . he had spoken of it before to many others. Now he singles out the daughters of his beloved Jerusalem. Maybe the women will listen. Maybe their devotion will save them.

The procession moves on down the street. But we are left wondering about what happened, about how magnificent the Lord was as he stopped the death squad by the sheer power of his person, about how he spoke to – *warned* – his daughters . . . yes, they are not only daughters of the holy city, they are ultimately *his* daughters.

Chapter Seven

A TIME TO DIVEST

> "But I, being poor, have only my dreams;
> I have spread my dreams under your feet;
> Tread softly because you tread on my dreams."
>
> – William Butler Yeats, 1899
> *He Wishes for the Cloths of Heaven*

The long trek from the judgment hall to the place of death is nearly complete. Looming ahead like a gray, weathered sentinel is the wall of Jerusalem. The street points straight toward the gate, flanked by towers to defend this access to the city. The sounds of animals and the jabbering of buyers and sellers identify the gate area as a marketplace.

Not far away are large pens crammed with sheep for the Passover sacrifices. Jesus, the Lamb of God on his way to slaughter, passes near the holding yard for the sacrificial animals. Hundreds of lambs will die in the temple, but Jesus will die outside the city – "outside the camp," as the writer of Hebrews will say (13:13).

As the procession nears the marketplace, the tenor of the talk changes sharply. Excited but good-natured bickering over prices turns to whispered questions concerning the condemned.

Out of the City

The steady pounding of the Roman drum is amplified

into terrible, hollow, reverberating thuds as the death squad passes through the structure that houses the gate. Cool darkness lasts only the few seconds it takes to slowly march through the passageway.

Now the treeless, sun-drenched landscape outside the gate assaults the eye. It's a cheerless scene – sad, anguished – a place that is sparse, hot, dry . . . oppressive.

City cobblestones give way to a hard-packed dirt road that relinquishes only small puffs of dust from the tromping feet. The crowds have thinned. Many have stopped in the narrow shade of the wall to watch the proceedings, now very visible in the open country. Their eyes follow the road ahead of the death squad to the place where it curves around a nasty little knoll. From there, it descends into the low country and disappears. Occasional morning travelers move along the austere thoroughfare, coming or going, unaware that they are passing the most profound event in history.

The procession arrives at the Place of the Skull. The crowd gathers around the hill while the soldiers and the condemned move up onto it. Among those standing by are relatives of the condemned, disciples of Jesus, curious onlookers, and, of course, a handful of religious leaders – chief priests, elders, teachers of the law.

The religious leaders feel duty-bound to ensure that "this blaspheming Jesus" is dispensed with once and for all. They're hoping to nip the situation in the bud. How could they know that they are, instead, scattering a billion seeds to the wind – seeds that will eventually fall onto fertile hearts in every corner of the earth, from this moment forward – as long as the earth stands.

Sounds of weeping and jeering intermingle. Tension rises, like that moment before the opening bell of a prize fight. Unseen angels lean closer – the portentous moment is very near now.

The soldiers go about their tasks in a rather mechanical and business-like manner. The three crosses that have been dragged to the hill are laid parallel to each other, with the bottom ends near the holes into which they soon will be dropped. The condemned are lined up, made to stand just beyond the tops of the crosses upon which they will die. Jesus is placed in the center; after all, he's become a celebrity of sorts, the reason for the larger-than-normal crowd.

So much attention has been focused on the central figure in this drama that we have almost forgotten that there are *three* men standing in a row, ready to die. Jesus, the innocent One, stands in the midst of guilt, between two criminals. Perhaps these two have worked this very road, assaulting and robbing travelers within a mile or two of this spot. Now they're paying for their crimes . . . with their lives.

Losing the Last Possession

The soldiers waste no time. To further humiliate the prisoners, they strip them of their clothing. When they come to Jesus, he too is reduced to nakedness. There's no place left for dignity. Except deep within the soul.

The Lord now faces the end of his earthly life, stripped of every temporal thing. It reminds us of Job, who, upon hearing of the last of the calamities to descend upon him (the death of his sons and daughters), said, "Naked I came from my mother's womb, and naked I will depart" (Job 1:21). As a matter of fact, Job was later restored to his former status and died surrounded by God's blessings. Jesus, however, *did* experience what Job had predicted for himself. Like all of us, Jesus came from his mother's womb naked. But unlike most of us, he is publicly stripped naked as his earthly life ends.

Once again, there is tremendous irony here. Jesus, the preexistent *Logos God*, left the riches and power of heaven behind when he became a human being. He himself created people – then he became like one of his creatures. As God in heaven, he had everything. As man on earth, he has nothing.

On one occasion, Jesus wanted a quiet time with his disciples, so he crossed to the other side of the lake from where the crowds were crushing in on him. But he was found there by a "teacher of the law" who came to him and said, "Teacher, I will follow you wherever you go."

Jesus replied, "Foxes have holes and birds of the air have nests, but the Son of Man has no place to lay his head" (Matthew 8:18-20).

Jesus meant that he had no permanent place to live on earth, no place to call home. But I wonder about the home in which he grew up, Joseph and Mary's home in Nazareth? Jesus was the eldest of the children, learning Joseph's trade, carpentry. When Joseph died, as he most likely did when Jesus was a teenager or young man, the house and the carpentry shop should have been bequeathed to Jesus, as custom required.

Apparently, when he began his ministry at about age 30, Jesus turned his back on all earthly inheritance. As he taught and preached, he lived by the generosity of his disciples. He stayed in the homes of people who loved him – Peter in Capernaum and Mary, Martha and Lazarus in Bethany, for example. But he himself owned no home. He accumulated no wealth. And shortly now, he will be buried in a borrowed tomb.

Jesus began with everything and ended with nothing. That's not exactly our definition of success today. In fact, it's the antithesis of it. In our world, success usually means starting with nothing and ending up with wealth or power – having it all. The opposite was true of Jesus, who gave and gave of his abundance – until there was nothing left to give, including his own blood.

As he faces death, Jesus isn't lying in a soft bed at

home, surrounded by family, giving a last will and testament that disposes of his possessions. He has nothing – nothing except the clothes on his back. And now that clothing is stripped from him. He will die as he was born . . . naked.

The humiliation is complete. The last thing he has on earth is taken from him. Now he has nothing.

Profits and Losses

In 2 Corinthians 8:9, we are told, "For you know the grace of the Lord Jesus Christ, that though he was rich, yet for your sakes he became poor, so that you through his poverty might become rich." Yet *even in his poverty*, he had what no one else ever had: an eternal identity! He was poor – but that wasn't his identity. He was humiliated – but that wasn't his identity. He was executed like the worst kind of criminal – but that wasn't his identity.

It should make us wonder why we tie our own identities so closely to our possessions, occupations, reputations, accomplishments – OR LACK OF THESE! We're *more* than our successes; and we also are *much more* than our failures. Why? Something inherent in us? No. It's only in Christ that we are more than our station or situation in life, because of the value Jesus places on us by dying for us.

At this moment, as Jesus' last meager possessions are stripped from him, we might take a moment to do a personal audit, a "balance sheet" that lists our profits and losses, our assets and liabilities. What do we count as a profit, what do we count as a loss?

Listen to the words of the apostle Paul: "But whatever was to my profit I now consider loss for the sake of Christ. What is more, I consider everything a loss compared to the surpassing greatness of knowing Christ Jesus my Lord, for whose sake I have lost all things. I consider them rubbish, that I may gain Christ and be found in him, not having a righteousness of my own that comes from the law, but that which is through faith in Christ – the righteousness that comes from God and is by faith."

But wait. We haven't heard Paul's conclusion.

"I want to know Christ," he says, "and the power of his resurrection and the fellowship of sharing in his sufferings, becoming like him in his death, and so, somehow, to attain to the resurrection from the dead" (Philippians 3:7-11). In his heart, Paul was there outside Jerusalem that day, stripped naked as the day he was born, suffering the beatings and insults, being nailed to the cross – "sharing in his sufferings, becoming like him in his death."

Where was Paul on the actual day Jesus was crucified? Nobody knows. Perhaps he was still studying in the great rabbinic schools. Or perhaps he was already teaching younger men the excellency of the Law of Moses. Wherever he was, he wasn't at Golgotha. He wasn't there among the religious leaders at the cross. But years later, after his astonishing conversion, he says, "I want to know Christ and . . . the fellowship of sharing in his sufferings, becoming like him in his death . . . ."

In his heart and mind, Paul placed himself there on Calvary with his Lord, he submitted to the humiliation, to the nakedness – he stretched out his hands to be crucified with his Lord. In his heart, he *was* crucified, nevertheless, he *lived* by faith in the risen Christ. And is not Paul an example for us of a faithful disciple of the Lord? Should we not also want to know Christ, to identify with his sufferings, to be like him in his death, so that we might also be like him in his resurrection?

In your mind, make two lists. At the top of one, write "Profits." At the top of the other put "Losses." Paul made such a list in his mind and described it for the

Philippians just before the last passage we noted. Here's what he listed as "Profits:"

1. Circumcised on the eighth day
2. Of the people of Iṣrael
3. Of the tribe of Benjamin
4. A Hebrew of Hebrews
5. In regard to the law, a Pharisee
6. As for zeal, persecuting the church
7. As for legalistic righteousness, faultless

(Philippians 3:5,6)

Those were all things that put him at the "top of the heap" in Jewish society. But in the next verse he says, "But whatever was to my profit I now consider loss . . . ." In effect, HE SWITCHED THE LISTS! He crossed out "Profits" and wrote in "Losses" over the seven points of pedigree and accomplishment. Then he crossed out "Losses," wrote in "Profits" . . . and under that heading wrote one word: CHRIST!

In this very complicated time, when we are swept along by strong tides of temptation and testing, Christians ought to continually check our profit and loss sheets. For, in the words of our Master, if we gain the whole world and lose our souls, what does it profit?

Naked Humiliation

Later, after their grisly work of crucifixion was done, the soldiers rummaged through the clothing of the crucified men. When they came to Jesus' garments, they divided them between the four soldiers assigned specifically to guard Jesus. But there was one garment left over – the tunic.

Every Jewish man had five articles of clothing: shoes, robe, sash, turban and tunic. The tunic was the undergarment. Over it was worn the robe, kept in place by the broad sash.

Soldiers were not well paid, so difficult duty such as serving on a crucifixion detail was compensated for by allowing the men to keep the condemned men's clothing. After each of the four soldiers had taken his choice of an article, they came to the fifth piece, the tunic. It had been woven as one cloth – there were no seams. Rather than tearing it into four parts and ruining it, the soldiers decided to gamble for it by casting lots.

Three of the gospel writers – Matthew, Mark and Luke – mention only that the soldiers gambled for Jesus' clothing. But John, who was the only eyewitness of the crucifixion among the writers, gives the greater detail. John tells us that the soldiers cast lots for only one of Jesus' garments – the tunic. He thought it so significant that John says, "This happened that the scripture might be fulfilled which said, 'They divided my garments among them and cast lots for my clothing.' So this is what the soldiers did" (John 19:24).

John even describes the tunic: "This garment was seamless, woven in one piece from top to bottom" (19:23). Some have suggested that it was an unusual undergarment, the kind worn by the high priest under his vestments. At the very least, John wants us to know that the whole incident is what King David prophesied about in his psalm when he sang, "Dogs have surrounded me; a band of evil men has encircled me, they have pierced my hands and my feet. I can count all my bones; people stare and gloat over me. They divide my garments among them and cast lots for my clothing" (Psalm 22:16-18).

"People stare and gloat over me," Jesus said through the mouth of David centuries before. People stare. The humiliation is very real. It's a *naked man* that is crucified, not one with a cloth wrapped artistically around his loins. Could we still accept the crucifixes, the paintings, the Bible School booklet illustrations if they correctly depicted the nakedness of Jesus? The cross is an interesting graphic design that lends itself to applications such as ornaments for church buildings and personal accessories. But it represents, not only the torturous death of our Lord, but also his naked humiliation.

Divesting and Investing

Jesus was stripped of his garments in preparation for his crucifixion. If we choose to identify with his suffering and death, as Paul did, then we too may need to be stripped of our "garments" – our possessions or reputation or position, the things that tie us to this world. We shouldn't fool ourselves into thinking that we're ready to "take up our cross and follow him" if we're not also ready to be stripped of our "garments."

As I return from the theology of the epistles to study the gospels, I'm amazed at the clarity, simplicity and power of Jesus' words. Those words take on added force because of the singular life he lived. Regarding the entanglements of this present world he said, "So do not worry, saying, 'What shall we eat?' or 'What shall we drink?' or 'What shall we wear?' For the pagans run after all these things, and your heavenly Father knows that you need them. But seek first his kingdom and his righteousness, and all these things will be given to you as well" (Matthew 6:31-33).

Jesus actually expects us to believe that statement. He actually suggests that we *not* "run after" all the things the pagans run after. But often we are indeed "running Christians," racing to get ahead, chasing power, position and possessions.

Jesus himself lived only to please the Father, and he expects his followers to do the same. He divested himself of heaven, then of all worldly attachments as he walked through the days of his ministry. And he expects us to divest ourselves, not necessarily of every material thing, but of every thing that distracts us substantially from living to the praise of our God.

How simply Jesus put it! "Do not store up for yourselves treasures on earth, where moth and rust destroy, and where thieves break in and steal. But store up for yourselves treasures in heaven, where moth and rust do not destroy, and where thieves do not break in and steal. For where your treasure is, there your heart will be also" (Matthew 6:19-21).

It's really a matter of the pride of ownership, the sense of security, the enjoyment of creature comforts, the satisfaction of accomplishment, the headiness of fame . . . over against dependence on God's grace and storing up treasures in heaven. Sometimes our "garments must be stripped away" in preparation for being "crucified with Christ." Humiliation always precedes glorification.

Now we stand at the base of this ugly hill, with our hearts in our throats. Golgotha does indeed look like a skull, with great gouges in the rocky earth that appear as dark eye sockets. Such an appropriate place for an execution. The grotesque mound adds to the feeling of death that hangs in the air.

The mood makes it seem like the dead of night, though it's barely day. The morning is warm; it will be hot soon. Our stomachs are in knots. We feel ill. Many shoulders shake with silent sobs. Some cry softly. But others in the crowd are hostile – they laugh and jeer – "they stare and gloat."

We look away as the soldiers roughly strip away the garments of our Lord. But though it breaks our hearts to see his shame and humiliation, we must turn back and be witnesses of it – for this too, is a lesson he teaches. In this humiliation, too, we may be called to follow.

Here he stands . . . despised, beaten, condemned,

without possessions . . . naked in the Judean sun. Yet, this naked man is not only the wisest and best of men, he's ultimately the richest of men in heaven's wealth. What lessons ought to surge through our hearts and minds as we see him there!

Chapter Eight

BEARING THE MARKS

"My sin – O the bliss of this glorious tho't –
My sin, not in part but the whole,
Is nailed to the cross and I bear it no more:
Praise the Lord, praise the Lord, O my soul!"

– Horatio G. Spafford, 1873

The energy and bustle of the city are but a few hundred yards away, yet they seem remote, distant. It's as if the world has drifted into suspended animation – the only thing happening is what is transpiring before us now. This is center stage; all else is backdrop.

The events on the rocky knoll are the focal point of heaven, as Deity and all spiritual beings lean near to watch the final scene that will change the relationship between God and man forever.

As always, there's a huge gulf between what people think is relevant and historical . . . and what God knows is ultimately important. Had satellite television news existed in this time, the reports would be coming in from around the world: political unrest and military skirmishes here, crop failures and weather-related disasters there. But it's almost certain that not even one television news crew would be covering the story that is unfolding outside the city wall of Jerusalem in this distant and minor Roman province. It's just another crucifixion – and crucifixions are not uncommon in this day, no more unusual than convictions and incarcerations of nameless felons in other times. The world doesn't notice as Jesus of Nazareth lays down his life on a Roman cross . . .

Death Chimes

That sound . . . suddenly we're conscious of it. We remember it vaguely from the procession along the city streets. It's a dull jangling sound, like discordant and ugly chimes.

Yes, now that we think about it, the jangling sound was there all the way from the garrison to the Place of the Skull, every step of the journey. Somehow, we didn't really pay any attention to it or identify it then, because of the terrible things that were happening. But now it comes back to us. The sound was there all along – eerie chimes, a sort of deathly music in cadence with the Roman drum.

The sound is coming from a basket carried by a man whom we remember. He had walked the entire way with the death squad. He isn't a soldier, and we thought it odd that he was allowed to walk with them. His clothing identifies him as a Jew, one of the despised collaborators who work for the Roman oppressors.

Now he moves across the knoll, stepping from the first cross to the second, then to the third. At each of the crosses, he pauses, reaches into his basket and withdraws four long, iron spikes. He drops them with a clatter into the dirt near the center of each cross.

That's the sound! That jangling of iron spikes is what we heard along the way. With a shudder we realize the nails were the death chimes.

The man returns to the first cross. He sets the basket down, pulls out a large hammer and stands patiently.

Meanwhile, the soldiers, who have been positioned around the perimeter of the hill by their centurion, allow some women into the execution area to give drink to the prisoners. These compassionate women have prepared a mixture of wine and gall (Matthew 27:34) or myrrh (Mark 15:23) that acts as a narcotic to deaden some of the pain of crucifixion. As the women move from one condemned man to the other, the two robbers eagerly gulp down large quantities of the bitter liquid, hoping to drink enough to take away the edge of the coming agony.

When the women come to Jesus, he takes only a sip, identifies it and rejects it. The women retreat down the slope to the crowd.

A few minutes pass. Then the centurion barks the command. Four soldiers quickly walk to the first prisoner. The condemned man begins to shout and sob; his facade of courage crumbles. The moment has come. He struggles violently, but he's no match for the soldiers who each grab an arm or leg and lift him bodily onto the nearby cross. While they pin the robber down, the man with the death chimes steps forward with his hammer. He drops to one knee, picks up a spike and pounds it through flesh into wood. Screams race to the city walls and echo back to mock the tortured man.

He and his cross are lifted upright by the soldiers, the base of the cross slips forward and drops into the hole with a jolt . . . and the deed is done. The soldiers return to their places on the perimeter, while the man continues to writhe in agony.

The centurion shouts again, and four other soldiers march the second robber forward. It's apparent now that the Roman officer is saving Jesus for last. In not much more than sixty seconds, the next condemned man is nailed to his cross, lifted and placed in position on the far end, leaving a vacant place between the two.

The enemies of Jesus are irritated by the delay. They yell their veiled insults at the centurion, who only looks away with a grim smile. He has already decided that his most famous prisoner is very different from others with whom he has dealt. This is a gentle, religious teacher, not an insurrectionist. The commander also has concluded that the Jewish leaders are motivated by a deadly jealousy. They want the popular, young teacher destroyed in order to protect their own positions of power over the common people.

The veteran Roman officer glances back and surveys the onlookers. Contempt burns in his eyes as his gaze sweeps across the crowd. "Look at these bloodthirsty fools," he thinks. "They're supposed to be *so religious*!" He shakes his head in disgust. "Even hand-to-hand combat doesn't prepare you for this kind of pettiness and hate. They're like sharks!"

When he has agitated the Jews enough by his delay, he finally shouts the command. There's no resistance from Jesus, no struggling, no pleading or sobbing. So, the four remaining soldiers simply accompany Jesus forward to his cross. He drops down quickly onto the wooden beams, stretches out his arms and the soldiers take hold of his hands and feet.

The repeated loud clang of metal against metal is heard across the bleak landscape . . . with great groans and labored breathing. But no pleading for himself. Instead, as he catches his breath, Jesus pleads for mercy for his executioners. Through clenched teeth of agony, he whispers, "Father, forgive them, for they do not know what they are doing" (Luke 23:34).

The centurion stares. Then he begins walking back and forth along the row of crosses with his hands clasped behind his back. He's heard the prayer of Jesus, but in all his years of military service, he's heard nothing like it. The words trouble him greatly.

Finally, the man with the death chimes steps back, his terrible work finished. The four soldiers lift the cross to a vertical position and let it slip into the socket with a sickening thud.

Jesus is nailed to the cross.

The Stigmata

This is the moment that we dread as Christians. It's the moment we've dreaded since we began this journey to the cross. Like the death of one who is very close to us – a wife or husband, a child, a mother or father, a brother or sister, a best friend – we're never quite prepared for it, even when we know it's imminent. Now, at this moment when the cross is a reality, we want to turn away, we want to run.

We're besieged daily by so many reports in the media of physical abuse, accidental deaths and terrible murders that we're often callous and unresponsive to such news. But when we hear that a beloved one is dead, we are overwhelmed with grief. What a difference when we *personally know* the person who died!

So it is with Christians who come to this scene at Calvary. The deeper our relationship with Christ, the more we are overcome with grief and shame . . . and the more we recoil at his torture and pain. We identify with him and want to cry out, "Stop, Lord, don't let it happen!"

But when we resign ourselves to the truth that there's no other way, we may find ourselves strangely drawn to Jesus, desiring to identify with him *completely*. We may even find ourselves saying, "Then let me die with you, Lord."

There are stories from past centuries that tell of the "Stigmata of Christ" – the marks of Christ. In these stories, people such as Francis of Assisi identify so intensely with Jesus that wounds appear in their hands and feet, wounds that correspond to Jesus' wounds on the cross.

Stigmata is a Latin word, plural of our word *stigma*.

Today, a stigma is "something that detracts from the character or reputation of a person, group, etc.; a mark of disgrace or reproach." Originally, however, stigma referred to a distinguishing mark burned or cut into the flesh of a slave or criminal – in other words, a *brand*, just like the ones we use on cattle even today.

In the early Christian era, stories began to circulate of people who had received the "marks of Christ" – his brand, if you will. Thus, the stigmata, originally the disgraceful sign of slavery, became the sign of grace and honor, marks bestowed by Christ on his beloved slaves.

Faithful people suddenly received wounds in their hands and feet, so the stories go, as they struggled in prayer and devotion – as they sought complete identification with the Savior. Jesus himself was said to have blessed them with his very own marks, as a sign of approval.

I certainly can't confirm – nor can I deny – those ancient stories. They have the weight of hundreds of years of tradition behind them. Who can say for sure whether they are fact or fiction? But I do know this: somehow every faithful Christian will eventually bear the marks of Jesus! Paul wrote an impassioned letter to the misled Galatian Christians, and he ended it by saying, "Finally, let no one cause me trouble, for I bear on my body the marks of Jesus" (Galatians 6:17).

What did Paul mean by that statement? Was he referring to the stigmata? Yes . . . in a sense. However, I don't believe Jesus burned wounds into Paul's hands and feet. That wasn't necessary, for Paul had plenty of marks that attested to his faithfulness to Christ. Just by following Jesus, Paul received in his body all kinds of abuses, and these were the "brand" of Christ, identifying Paul as a chosen servant of the Lord.

When he wrote to the Corinthian Christians, Paul reminded them that he "had been in prison more frequently, been flogged more severely, and been exposed to death again and again." Five times he received 39 lashes from the Jews. Three times he was beaten with rods. Once they tried to stone him to death. On and on he listed the "marks of Jesus" on his body (2 Corinthians 11:23-29).

Earlier in that letter, Paul had said, "For just as the sufferings of Christ flow over into our lives, so also through Christ our comfort overflows" (2 Corinthians 1:5). Think about that statement once again: the sufferings of Christ flow over into our lives. Paul took it for granted that Christ's sufferings would overflow to us, and he wanted to encourage us with the promise that "through Christ, our comfort overflows" also.

So, how about us? Do we bear on our bodies the marks of Jesus? Have his sufferings come upon us? Do we have the *stigmata*? If not, should we rejoice – or should we wonder if we have truly identified with the suffering, crucified Lord?

Fair Weather Christians

I sometimes wonder if many of us who call ourselves Christians are really only "fair weather" disciples. We're faithful and joyful followers when surrounded by relative peace and prosperity. But what do we do when really tough times assail us? Do we shrink back and cry, "Lord, where are you? How can you let this happen to me? Haven't I tried to live a faithful and obedient life? Why are you punishing me – allowing this to happen?"

There are disciples who, under such pressure, turn back and walk in the way no more. Somewhere, some of us have gotten the idea that only Jesus is supposed to suffer, and if we'll just believe in him, no evil will come to us.

Multitudes love the idea of a resurrected Christ, even if they don't believe in him – because everybody loves a winner. But what about the Jesus who is nailed to the cross? Do we rush on past that terrible, embarrassing, scandalous moment – and try to avoid the crucified Jesus?

Pop psychology and human thinking have invaded some of our churches and pulpits to the point that something as "negative" as the bloody sacrifice of Jesus on the cross is avoided, replaced by positive platitudes. But if people despise the bloody cross, then they despise Jesus, because that is his supreme moment – the moment for which he was born.

The masses love "baby Jesus" at Christmastime. The Jesus in the manger. And they love the Jesus who teaches morality and non-violence, who resists religious hypocrisy. They love the Jesus who performs miracles. But none of that matters if they don't love the blood of Christ – his substitutionary death, his sacrifice – and the demands that makes on each of us.

I believe that, somewhat like Francis of Assisi and the stigmata of Jesus, the more we struggle to understand the sacrifice of Christ, the more we will feel bound to identify with him in his sufferings. As we meditate on those nails in his hands and feet, as we really consider that historical moment when man tried to kill God, we will realize that his sufferings *flow over to us*. We will feel the nails in our own hands and in our own feet, perhaps not in a physical sense, but in a deeply spiritual sense.

It's not easy for the person who loves Jesus to look upon his suffering with the eye of imagination. We cringe and want to look away. It hurts to look at his pain – it hurts terribly. But maybe it is *supposed* to hurt. Maybe we *need* to hurt more often . . . in order to be changed and transformed into his image.

The Tree-maker on His Tree

Look again toward that ghastly knoll that is shaped

like a skull. Above the figures of the soldiers we now see two crosses rising – with two men hanging in excruciating pain. Between them is a third man, still on the ground, pinned down on top of his cross. The man with the hammer raises it high above his head, and in one swift motion, brings it crashing down on a spike held against one of Jesus' hands.

Clang! The echoing, metallic sound is followed immediately by an instinctive spasm and guttural groan – a shaking, a twisting in pain, a gasping for air. Seconds later, it happens again. Clang! Then again . . . .

The blows are felt in our own hands and feet. We ache. We grieve. We experience the tilting motion, and with Jesus we watch through narrow eyes the blue sky swing down to a landscape of watching faces. We feel the jarring, tearing jerk as the cross hits the bottom of the socket with a sudden stop. With Jesus, we feel the warm blood trickle down our arms, drip off our feet. Death hovers all around us.

Now we are struck by the full force of the fact that this man on the center cross is not just a good man or the best man . . . he is the Son of the Living God. And men, representatives of us all, have nailed the Son of God to a tree.

It was this Son of God who *created* the tree upon which he now hangs; he made the iron of the spikes and hammer; he even made the soldiers and the jeering high priests. For this is the Creator God, himself made in human form . . . hanging on a cross.

Chapter Nine

LIFTED UP

"When I survey the wondrous cross
On which the Prince of glory died,
My richest gain I count but loss
And pour contempt on all my pride."

– Isaac Watts, 1707

It's only 9 a.m. The eastern sun is making its ascent into a cloudless sky . . . and we wonder how hot it will be when it's this warm already.

The earliest chores are finished for many people in the city and surrounding villages, and now they are settling into their morning labor. But for Jesus, these early hours are climaxing an ordeal that has lasted through an endless, sleepless night. While others were eating their breakfast of bread, cheese and olives, he was being beaten with fists and bone-studded leather strips. While others were beginning their daily work, he was forcing his fatigued body forward under the weight of a wooden cross.

It's 9 a.m. And we think of all the things a person might anticipate at this hour: Passover preparations, plans for visiting with relatives, a tasty meal, sharing a game or hobby with a friend, getting ready for the Sabbath. Thousands of things, so many life-affirming things – other than watching one's life ebb away.

It will be over in six hours – 360 agonizing minutes,

each minute containing 60 seconds of searing pain. It will seem like an eternity.

With the three men crucified, the centurion gives his soldiers the order to stand at ease. "And sitting down, they kept watch over him there" (Matthew 27:36).

There's one very distinctive thing about the center cross as it is silhouetted against the city. Jesus' cross has a sign above his head affixed to the upper part of the vertical beam. The message on the sign is written in three languages – in the local Aramaic, in the Latin of the Romans, and in the more universal Greek tongue. It reads, "THIS IS JESUS OF NAZARETH, THE KING OF THE JEWS."

It was common for the Romans to attach a sign to a cross to notify passersby of the crimes of the crucified one. What significance is associated with this particular message above the Savior's head! The Roman governor, Pilate, ordered it lettered in three languages so *everyone* would know this man's offense. And what is the offense? He's King of the Jews!

The Romans had a good laugh and enjoy the ingenious and insulting twist. Pilate was delighted when the chief priests came screaming to him as they saw the sign! "Do not write 'The King of the Jews,' but that this man *claimed* to be King of the Jews," they cried out (John 19:21).

But with satisfaction and a barely-concealed smile, Pilate answered, "What I have written, I have written." To himself, he may have said, "What a brilliant move! I labeled it a crime to be 'King of the Jews.' At the same time, I embarrassed and angered these pompous chief priests who want the rabbi killed. They got what they wanted; but everyone who passes Golgotha will see that we've executed the King of the Jews!"

The Center Cross

The minutes creep by imperceptibly, while the road that leads by Golgotha increases in foot traffic. Some of the travelers stop, read the sign, ask a question or two, then take up an ignorant tirade. "You who are going to destroy the temple and build it in three days, save yourself!" they shout as they wag their heads. "Come down from the cross, if you are the Son of God!" (Matthew 27:39,40).

Where did they get such taunts? Did these passersby know about Jesus? Did they remember his statement about the temple – and are they now throwing it back at him? Perhaps. But it's more likely that they've asked about "The King of the Jews," and the gloating but agitated religious leaders have recounted to them of how Jesus said, "Destroy this temple, and I will raise it again in three days" (John 2:19).

It was at an earlier Passover, perhaps three years ago, that the leaders had asked Jesus for a miraculous sign to prove he had the authority to drive the profiteers from the temple. The only sign he gave them was to foretell this present event. Jesus spoke of the crucifixion and resurrection of his own body, of course, not the destruction and rebuilding of the temple in Jerusalem. But they didn't understand.

Now these chief priests, teachers of the law and elders all join in the mockery. "He saved others, but he can't save himself!" they yell. "He's the King of Israel! Let this Christ come down now from the cross, and we will believe in him. He trusts in God. Let God rescue him now if he wants him, for he said, 'I am the Son of God'" (Matthew 27:41-43; Luke 23:35).

Their sneering rebukes reveal that they have learned much about Jesus: that he cleansed the temple; that he talked of the destruction and rebuilding of "this temple;" that he was called the Son of God; that he trusted in God; that he was referred to as the King of Israel and the Messiah. They know much. But they don't know enough. It's like some religious leaders and theologians in our own day who reject the Deity of Christ. They, too, know much about Jesus – but they don't know enough. In fact, they don't really know him at all.

Once again the soldiers take up their mockery. "Save yourself," they yell at Jesus. But their chiding is somehow different than that of the Jews. The soldiers mock the Jews, as well as Jesus. The whole thing is a macabre joke to the Romans. "These intolerant fanatics who kill teachers they don't agree with," they are saying, "these petty, feuding religious bigots . . . what fools the Hebrews are. What a wretched land this is!"

All of them – travelers on the road, onlookers, chief priests, teachers of the law, elders, soldiers – they all heap abuse on the only innocent One among them. And now, even one of the crucified robbers joins the jeering. "Aren't you the Christ? Save yourself and us!" he shouts in gasps (Luke 23:39-43).

But from the other cross comes a very different attitude, very different words. He looks beyond Jesus to the bitter man and says, "Don't you fear God, since you are under the same sentence? We are punished justly, for we are getting what our deeds deserve. But this man has done nothing wrong."

Then a remarkable thing happens. The full impact of what is transpiring seizes the robber with the new-found compassion and faith. The first man challenges Jesus saying, "Aren't you the Christ," but the second man calls Jesus by name and acknowledges his power and authority. "Jesus," he says as the tears come, "remember me when you come into your kingdom."

Jesus turns his head slowly, looks at the man and whispers, "I tell you the truth, today you will be with me in paradise" (Luke 23:39-43).

Three men on crosses – representing the destiny of the world. In the center is the One who offers himself as a ransom for sin, a way of escape from the condemnation that grips us all. On one side is a man who represents the rejection of that sin offering; he's the cynic who wants to be saved but hasn't the power to trust. But on the other side is the man who represents those who trust, who don't know how or why or when, but say, "Jesus, remember me when you come into your kingdom. Remember me . . . ."

All men and women are on the three crosses. On the center cross is the "New Man," the God Man, the Savior. On one side is the "Old Man" who rejects the Savior. And on the other side is the "Old Man" who receives Jesus and is transformed into a "New Man" like his Savior. Every person is on one side or the other – the future of all humanity is thus pictured on the three crosses of Golgotha.

In the final analysis, the *only hope* for us and for all people is identification with the center cross. Christ is the one source of new life, and we must be united with him – "Christ in us, the hope of glory." We must, in fact, "cling to the old rugged cross," for as strange as it may seem, that cross, which is the very picture of death, is the only source of future life and glory.

The Holiest Place on Earth

Beyond the jeering crowd is the group of followers of Jesus. Then, a little apart from them is the handful of grief-stricken women who are being comforted and supported by a young man. There's Mary, the wife of Clopas (or Cleopas) – her husband may be one of the two men who, later, meet the Lord on the road to Emmaus. Also in the little group is Mary from Magdala, perhaps the most remarkably converted person among the early disciples. Jesus' aunt is there (or perhaps she is a second cousin), standing on one side to strengthen Jesus' mother; and on the other side, with his arm tightly around the woman between them, is John, Jesus' closest friend among the disciples. The obvious center of the huddled disciples is Mary, the mother of Jesus.

The warmth of the morning and the passing of time take their toll on the people. Gradually, those who are merely curious drift back toward the city gate or on to some other destination. This allows the disciples to move closer to their Lord.

John nervously approaches the centurion and asks if he and Jesus' mother may stand closer to the center cross. The officer glances out at Mary, sweeps the crowd with his eyes for any potential danger, then nods. He sees no reason why the dying man shouldn't be allowed to see his mother. John carefully helps Mary up the rocky path. A few dozen steps and they are there . . . at the foot of the cross.

It is the most awesome spot on the surface of the earth, there at the foot of the cross. It is a holy place beyond words. It is the archetype of the "mercy seat," that cover which laid atop the ark of the covenant, that place where the blood of animals was sprinkled in the Holy of Holies. This is the TRUE mercy seat where the blood of God's TRUE Lamb is poured out. The magnificent temple in Jerusalem, for all its adornment, was simply a poor precursor or shadow of what is happening here at the cross.

At this moment, priests are going about their duties and preparing for the Passover Sabbath. But none of them realizes that, outside the city, the TRUE PASSOVER IS HAPPENING! We want to go there and shout, "Listen, you priests of God! Come outside of the city to the true Passover, to the true temple, to the true Paschal lamb!"

Do Mary and John know they are standing at the very

pivotal point of history . . . standing where millions upon millions of believers will, by faith, someday stand . . . where you and I stand at this very moment by faith?

Imagine it. They are *there* at the holiest place, not just of that time, but of all of history – at the foot of Jesus' cross! The Holy of Holies in the temple was so sacred that *only* the high priest could enter it – and then *only* once a year. But here is the true moment of atonement, *open for all eyes to see*! But few are looking, no one really understands.

What a strange mixture of emotions flood in on us as we gaze upon the crucified Son of God: the shame, the exaltation, the pity, the adoration, the revulsion, the gratitude, the fear, the awe, the joy, the pain . . . the utter amazement and reverence!

Jesus opens his eyes to narrow slits, sees his mother, then blinks the sweat and dust aside. His mother's kind mouth quivers, but she cannot speak. Instead, after a moment of silence, Jesus himself speaks. "Dear woman," – his parched voice is strained and hoarse – "here is your son." His eyes move and finally rest on John.

Then to John he says, "Here . . . is your mother."

John looks at Mary. As he turns back toward Jesus he nods – but doesn't speak. He knows what's being asked. He knows what's required. He's making a lifetime commitment to care for the mother of his Lord. No contracts or promises are necessary. It's done. From that moment, Mary will live in John's home, until the moment she joins her son – her Lord – in his paradise.

Darkness to Match the Deed

The sun has now reached its zenith, and only the most bitter of Jesus' enemies remain as the rocky hill begins to broil in the noonday heat. The condemned men already are burned red from three hours of nakedness in the sun. As fevers begin to rise, fueled by pain, shock and heat, they feel as though they're on fire.

Then suddenly at the brightest and hottest point of the day, the sunlight begins to fade. Is it a passing cloud bringing a few minutes of welcomed shade and relief? No. The sky is cloudless. Somehow, the sun itself seems to be dimming. Impossible! As we watch, it changes moment by moment . . . faster and faster. Hardly a minute has gone by, and it's becoming as night.

The centurion quickly calls out to two of his men, and the pair race into the city to fetch torches. The other soldiers clutch their spears and shields tightly, close ranks to an arms-length formation around the three crosses.

The darkness brings a sudden chill to the air, and the temperature of heated bodies plummets. The stillness makes one aware of the faint sound of lambs bleating in the distance. Instinctively, everyone lowers his or her voice; some quietly joke about the crazy weather and the inconvenience – trying hard to swallow the fear that tightens their throats.

Tiny points of light – candles and torches – begin to appear in the city. Doors are being bolted. The city gates are creaking shut. And still it grows darker – like the blackest, starless night.

Old-timers in the city are telling tales of eclipses they've experienced in their vast lifetimes, yet even they are edgy, watchful with darting eyes. Everyone is listening . . . waiting . . . watching the inky nothingness . . . .

Several minutes pass. The two soldiers can be seen returning from the city gates. They appear as dancing lights in the darkness that grow larger as they approach. A few seconds later and we can see the flames of the torches trailing behind as they run along the road toward us.

They reach Golgotha and quickly light and distribute the other torches they're carrying. The flickering flames make the scene surreal, as grotesque and satanic as it actually is. This whole ordeal of Jesus – from arrest and trial to condemnation and cross – is *a deed of darkness*, committed by means of an unholy alliance between the Jews and the Romans. Now Almighty God plunges the world into a darkness to match the deed. Men grope in sightless sin – and now they grope in physical darkness, as well.

The centurion paces back and forth, his short-sword swinging at his side. Years of experience in countless battles and skirmishes have taught him to smell danger, anticipate the enemy, sense when things are wrong. As he ponders the past four or five hours, many things have troubled him. Even before the darkness descended, he was wary and tense. Now the blackness confirms his apprehension. "It's all wrong. It didn't feel right from the beginning," he reflects. "I wonder what's next?"

He stops pacing in front of the center cross and stares up at Jesus. He's sure that Jesus is somehow behind the bizarre occurrences of the day. "Who are you? You're not like the others," he may be thinking. "There's something about you that sets you apart from these petty criminals. And you're not like these small men who call themselves 'Elders of Israel.' I'm in command here, but you have some kind of unearthly power. Who are you, Jesus of Nazareth?"

The Price is Paid

The torches illuminate the twisted figure of Jesus with orange-yellow light and reveal the horror etched in his face. The two other crucified men also are in physical agony – but there's something infinitely deeper about the suffering of Jesus. He writhes with pain that's beyond the torture of the gaping wounds in his hands and feet, the puncture wounds on his head, and the cuts and welts on his back. In fact, his face has an other-worldly contortion about it. In truth he is, at this very moment, experiencing the unthinkable horror of human guilt . . . not as I experience my guilt or you experience yours. He is experiencing ALL HUMAN GUILT – becoming guilty of all human sin, from the Garden of Eden down to the final generation of people, whenever that will be. He who is the personification of love now becomes the personification of sin. And he experiences the punishment for that sin and guilt.

With every passing minute that creeps by, the anxiety increases, because there's no apparent reason for this blackness at midday. Darkness at the end of day brings welcome rest from one's labors. But unexplained darkness in the middle of day strikes fear into the heart.

An hour finally passes. And another. "Will it never end?" the centurion wonders.

The mocking has long since ceased. Even talk among the soldiers has dwindled to almost nothing. Quietness reigns on the hill.

Suddenly, loud Aramaic words shatter the silence! A pitiful but frightening scream makes everyone's flesh crawl.

"Eloi, Eloi, lama sabachthani?" is the cry from the center cross.

The centurion's heart is pounding wildly! He walks quickly to the edge of the hill. "What did he say?" he demands of the few Jewish leaders who remain.

"He said, 'My God, my God, why have you forsaken me?'" answers the man who stands nearest. But others, who are a little farther away, have misunderstood. "Listen, he's calling Elijah," they tell one another. When Jesus cried out, "Eloi" (my God), they thought he said, "Elijah" (the name of the great prophet of God whom many thought would return to Israel one day).

In the flickering light, every eye is trained on Jesus now.

After a moment, Jesus raises his head and says quietly, "I thirst."

"I don't understand," thinks the centurion. "He has such spiritual power, yet now he's convinced that he has been forsaken by his God." To one of the onlookers, he orders, "Give him a drink!"

The man runs and grabs a sponge, dips it into a bowl of wine vinegar, affixes the sponge to a stick and lifts it to Jesus' mouth. Although Jesus had rejected the drugged wine earlier, he now accepts the wine vinegar to moisten his parched lips and mouth. The man with the sponge steps back and someone shouts, "Now leave him alone. Let's see if Elijah comes to take him down" (Mark 15:33-36).

Revived for a second, Jesus opens his eyes slightly and takes in the scene from his vantage point . . . for the last time. He sees all eyes quietly staring at him. Perhaps he thinks, "You have lifted me up on this tree. If only you would lift me up in your hearts. Even in my death, *you must look up to me* – but you don't understand. This is as it is meant to be. Someday every one of you, every person in every age, will bow before me and look up in awe. Why won't you bow in faith now, before it is too late?"

The pain rushes in on him with a vengeance. It's time to depart. He has completed the work he was sent to do. The price – the unspeakable price – has been paid.

His eyes close, and with thin breath he says, "It is finished. Father, into your hands I commit my spirit."

His head drops heavily onto his chest. The last gasp of air from his lungs rushes out.

He is dead.

Black Chaos

The centurion has been watching intently and is immediately troubled. In the torch light, he glances from side to side, toward the other crosses. The men who flank Jesus are suffering terribly, but they're still very much alive, and the officer knows they'll continue to suffer for many hours, even days, unless their deaths are quickened somehow.

"What's going on?" he no doubt is thinking. "This Jesus is no weakling. But he just bowed his head and died . . . as if he *chose* to die. Amazing!"

The thought has barely raced through his mind when the Roman is startled by a rumbling sound, like distant thunder. The sound grows louder, becomes a vibration. He doesn't even have time to shout an order to his men. Before he can prepare himself, the earth is pitching and shaking. Rocks shatter, dust rises in the wildly dancing torch light. It looks like a scene from hell itself!

Everyone is thrown to the ground – it's impossible to stand upright. People cover their heads as the earth undulates with an ear-splitting roar. Most of the torches have been dropped or thrown, and the hill is once again engulfed in darkness.

In the black chaos, some of the Jewish people are beating their breasts, crying, trying to run, stumbling, falling. Is it . . . the end of the world?

These people trembling in fear at dark Golgotha will find out soon that, at this very moment, the huge curtain in the temple is ripping from top to bottom. Outside the city walls, many of the tombs in the cemeteries, even those cemeteries near Golgotha, are cracking open, the dead are coming to life and walking the streets of Jerusalem.

Nature has gone berserk! But you must understand . . . the Son of the Living God has died!

The rolling earth relaxes. The rumbling trails off into the distance. There's enough light to trace the outline of Calvary . . . the darkness is retreating.

Stillness.

In a matter of seconds, the sun has returned to full strength. But it has dropped into the afternoon sky. It's about 3 p.m. – the blackness has ruled for three hours.

Now we hear them. For the first time since the sun began to fade, the birds are singing again in the trees and bushes a hundred yards away.

The centurion is transfixed. He stands looking at the lifeless body of Jesus on the cross, and fresh images of the past few hours flash through his mind. His soldiers are shaken by the strange events, but the officer himself has taken inventory of the drama and all the participants. Without removing his gaze from the center cross, he says out loud, "Surely he was the Son of God!"

Sustained by Sacrifice

We don't have stone altars anymore. Nor temples with golden altars. We don't offer bulls, goats, sheep, doves, and other animals on altars of any kind. And perhaps because of that, the concept of sacrifice has lost much of its meaning for us. But we must never, never forget that this world moves forward *only through sacrifice*. That is the way God created it. It will work no other way.

Infants come into the world through the sacrifice and, yes, the blood of their mothers. Without sacrifice, the growing infants will die. Families survive physically and emotionally through the sacrifice of parents. Law and order and personal safety are maintained through the sacrifice of police officers, firefighters and many others. Heroes are remembered and emulated because they sacrificed themselves for other people.

The world is sustained by sacrifice. And as sacrifice becomes more scarce, as it becomes something only to be received and not to be offered of oneself, the world will grind to a halt. It cannot continue without enormous amounts of sacrifice.

How can a horrid, bloody instrument of torture and death become a thing of beauty? "O that old rugged cross, so despised by the world, Has a wondrous attraction for me," goes the old song. The gruesome cross becomes lovely because of the sacrifice of Jesus Christ. Earth is meaningless without a heaven, and heaven is accessible only through his sacrifice.

Jesus knew so well that the cross would come to him – or rather, that he would go to it. He said, "Just as Moses lifted up the snake in the desert, so the Son of Man must be lifted up, that everyone who believes in him may have eternal life" (John 3:14,15). Without knowing it, the Romans fulfilled the prophecy of Jesus by actuating the event foreshadowed by Numbers 21:6-9. They *lifted Jesus up* on a cross. They played into God's hands – he used them to fulfill his sovereign will. Jesus said, "But I, when I am lifted up from the earth, will draw all men to myself" (John 12:32). And now it happens just as he said it would.

Below his cross are both Jews and Gentiles – "all [kinds of] men." On either side of Jesus are the representatives of "all [types of] men," a believer and an unbeliever. They are all drawn to Calvary, where Jesus is lifted up by the Romans, by the Jews, by the believers, by the unbelievers, by you, by me . . . by God. The Messiah is the center of the universe, and though they hadn't planned it so, all men look up to Jesus. When we come to this place at the foot of the cross, we *must* look up . . . because the cross is always above us.

He Understands

And yet, as we are compelled to look up, it is Jesus' pleasure to look down on *our* suffering in infinite compassion. He's very aware that each of us will one day face death. It may come to us in an instant or in a protracted ordeal, but it will surely come. In our secret, unguarded moments, most of us wonder what death will be like. But here at the cross of Christ there is a comforting thought for us. No one could take the life of Jesus, yet he *gave it willingly*. Jesus died! He experienced death – the worst kind of death. So he understands our apprehension about the pain and the finality of it all – he's been there.

As Henry Lyte faced his own death in 1847, he wrote these wonderful words: "Hold Thou Thy cross before my closing eyes; Shine through the gloom, and point me to the skies; Heav'n's morning breaks, and earth's vain shadows flee; In life, in death, O Lord, abide with me!"

And Jesus *will* abide with us in life . . . and in death. Because he knows what it is to look into the yawning mouth of death as it prepares to swallow us. He knows. He cares. We are not alone.

"It is finished," he says. The debt is finished, OUR DEBT IS PAID! But the pathway we now walk isn't yet finished. It won't be finished until the magnificent vindication of Christ, the glorious resolution of this death on the cross.

For now, gaze once more at the three crosses that rise above the barren hill outside Jerusalem. The center cross is a little higher than the ones on either side. The Romans wanted it to stand out. They had no idea that they were lifting up the Savior of the world and that he would draw all men to himself. The centurion was right –Jesus our Lord was, AND IS, the Son of God!

In the early morning sun, in the noonday heat, in the thick darkness, in the earthquake . . . there, before an uncaring world . . .

Jesus dies.

But glory is now very close at hand.

Chapter Ten

CHALLENGE OF OBEDIENCE

"O Captain! my Captain! our fearful trip is done,
The ship has weathered every rack,
the prize we sought is won,
The port is near, the bells I hear,
the people all exulting."

– Walt Whitman, 1892
O Captain! My Captain!

Jesus is the greatest of blessings to those who love him. But he can be a very real problem to those who don't. During his years on earth, for example, he was a source of irritation, frustration and, finally, bitter hatred for the Jewish leaders. Now, in his death, he is still a problem for them.

It occurs to these leaders that the special Sabbath is near – a holy day to Yahweh – and three people are hanging on crosses near one of the city's gates. The crucified men will defile the Sabbath, they decide. Perhaps they are thinking of the passage in Leviticus 21:10,11 that says, "The high priest . . . must not enter a place where there is a dead body." Or maybe they're considering Numbers 5:1,2 that says, "The Lord said to Moses, 'Command the Israelites to send away from the camp anyone who . . . is ceremonially unclean because of a dead body.'"

The events of the last few hours have the leaders nervous and agitated. The afternoon sun is shining again, as if nothing unusual had ever happened. All seems normal now. But for three hours, Jerusalem was shrouded in darkness – at what should have been the brightest point of the day. Then at the end of the blackness, an earthquake rattled everyone to the bone. Damage reports are still coming in on the tragedy. Already, bizarre stories of dead people rising to life are circulating in the city. There are also initial reports of heavy damage to the temple.

Tunnel-vision Can Kill

Getting rid of Jesus should have been such an easy matter. Instead, this day has turned into a nightmare for the religious leaders. The talk at the city gate near Golgotha has it that even the Roman centurion himself acknowledged that Jesus was, in fact, the Son of God. "Is there no end to the trouble this man will bring us?" is probably the discussion among Jesus' enemies.

So, the immediate task is to get rid of the bodies of Jesus and the two thieves before the beginning of the holy Sabbath. The leaders rush through the streets of Jerusalem, back to the Roman governor. "They asked Pilate to have the legs broken and the bodies taken down" (John 19:31).

Their request seems to be a vivid example of the twisted thinking even "religious people" are capable of. These leaders of God's nation ostensibly want to obey the laws of God, so they decide to whisk away the "unclean" bodies they themselves have made unclean (with the help of the Romans) by crucifixion. They murder Jesus and are then concerned that his dead body may contaminate their religious service! They want to "clean up their mess," in a manner of speaking, before the beginning of God's holy Sabbath.

The humiliation, the floggings, the torture and the crucifixions are not enough. They now want the Romans to break the legs of the crucified – six legs to be exact –

to speed death so the bodies can be removed. The leaders could have ended the lives of the condemned with one swift blow, but even now, a merciful death is denied.

When their legs are broken, the men will hang from the crossbar by their nailed hands. They will be unable to push up with their legs to relieve the pressure against their lungs and catch their breath – they will suffocate. Death will come, not only with pain, but with that horrible panic that accompanies the inability to breathe. This is the choice of the religious leaders: to "please God," they will further torture the doomed men.

How can they imagine that God will be pleased with such a brutal course of action? It is a religious tunnel-vision that prompts the terrible request. They look narrowly at some Levitical law, some statute of Moses perhaps, and fail to see the true character of God – his mercy, his compassion, his love for even the vilest person. The leaders conclude that "obedience" to God justifies terrible abuse to some of God's creation. The lesson is that tunnel-vision can end in sin, in tragedy, even in torture and murder.

And before we become too judgmental, we might want to remind ourselves that the tunnel-vision of church leaders or ordinary Christians today can kill the enthusiasm, the spirit, the faith in people's hearts . . . can kill relationships among God's people – all in the name of God.

Fulfilling Prophecy

When the Jewish leaders return with the official approval of Pontius Pilate, the centurion passes the order on to his men. The soldiers proceed to the first cross and methodically carry out the command.

How do they break the man's legs? We can't be sure. But whether it is by using a lever or by a swift blow from a club, great force has to be applied – severe trauma is inflicted on a living human being. As we consider that cruel action – indeed, the whole crucifixion process – we may find it difficult to consider the Romans and Jews of that time civilized people.

The soldiers walk past Jesus to the cross on the other side. The gruesome deed is done again, with the same nauseating sound and the same pitiable screams, followed by the same great gaspings for air.

Finally, the soldiers move to the center cross. They are already quite sure that Jesus is dead. He hasn't moved for some time.

"Strange," they are thinking, "that Jesus should die so quickly, before the others."

"No sense in breaking this one's legs," says one soldier.

Another warrior agrees. But then he steps forward, lifts his spear. "He seems to be dead, but we must take no chances . . ." he says as he draws back his shaft. Uncoiling his powerful upper body, he thrusts the spear deep into Jesus' side, "bringing a sudden flow of blood and water" (John 19:34).

Several explanations have been advanced by scholars that give medical answers as to why separated blood and water flowed from Jesus' side. How it happened medically may not be as important as *why* it happened. The apostle John was quite specific in his description; he wanted us to know exactly what happened.

Many years later as an old man – and perhaps as he languishes in exile – John remembers the blood and water that flowed from the Lord's side. He may be thinking how symbolic, how prophetic it is, and he writes, "This is the one who came by water and blood – Jesus Christ. He did not come by water only, but by water and blood. And it is the Spirit who testifies, because the Spirit is the truth. For there are three that testify: the Spirit, the water and the blood; and the three are in agreement" (1 John 5:6-8).

Not only is John impressed by the water and the blood, but he also is amazed by the whole sequence of events, and he records the incident of the breaking of the bones. He says, "The man who saw it [speaking of himself] has given testimony, and his testimony is true. He knows that he tells the truth, and he testifies so that you also may believe" (John 19:35). He wants us to know that these are not fanciful tales.

Then he adds, "These things happened so that the scripture would be fulfilled: 'Not one of his bones will be broken,' and, as another scripture says, 'They will look on the one they have pierced'" (John 19:36,37). John seems to refer to the Passover story and, specifically, to the instruction from God regarding the preparation of the Passover lamb: "It [the Passover meal] must be eaten inside one house; take none of the meat outside the house. Do not break any of the bones" (Exodus 12:46).

This seems such a strange instruction from God! In the eating of the lamb – and even in the slaughtering process, I presume – what difference does it make if one of the lamb's bones is broken? To the Israelites, the instruction probably appeared ridiculous or even superstitious. But this wasn't an ordinary lamb feast. It was sacred, special. Holy to the holy God.

What difference does it make if a bone is broken? What difference does it make if Noah's ark is exactly 450 feet long and 75 feet wide? What difference does it make if the ten tabernacle curtains are exactly 28 cubits by 4 cubits? What difference does it make if the Lord's Supper includes wine and bread, and not olives and cheese? What difference do any of the specific instructions of the Lord make? The short answer is, it's a matter of obedience to the Sovereign Creator.

More specifically, in God's scheme of things, there are important relationships that exist between people, actions and events, even though those things may be separated by time and space. God decrees something as apparently meaningless as not breaking a lamb's bones, and many hundreds of years later, Roman soldiers break the bones of the men on either side of Jesus – but when they come to him, they pierce his side but do not break a single bone. And the young apostle John, standing near the hill of Calvary, notices, remembers . . . and finally writes, "These things happened so that the scripture would be fulfilled: 'Not one of his bones will be broken.'" God is weaving a tapestry across history, and every woof and warp are meaningful when one steps back and views the artwork from afar.

The Jews asked Pilate to order the breaking of bones, but God had already said of his Passover lamb, "Do not break any of the bones." The Mosaic Passover lamb was only a prophetic shadow of the true sacrificial lamb of God – Jesus himself – whose blood covers the faithful who flee to him for refuge.

Those early Israelites had no notion that, in obeying God in the Passover meal, they were picturing a momentous future event. They were foreshadowing this place on the way of the cross where we now stand – where the plans of men are thwarted by the decree of God – "Not one of his bones will be broken."

The apostle John also sees the fulfillment of another Old Testament passage in the events after Jesus' death. In Zechariah 12:10, God says,

> And I will pour out on the house of David and the inhabitants of Jerusalem a spirit of grace and supplication. They will look on me, the one they have pierced, and they will mourn for him as one mourns for an only child, and grieve bitterly for him as one grieves for a firstborn son.

John never forgets the moment when the soldier shoves

the spear into Jesus' side. Years later on the island of Patmos, he prophesies about an earthshaking time to come: "Look, he is coming with the clouds, and every eye will see him, even those who pierced him, and all the people of the earth will mourn because of him. So shall it be! Amen" (Revelation 1:7).

A Bold Request

Perhaps it happened something like this . . .

"There's a Jew at the gate, sir, and he's requesting an audience with you," the attendant says to Pontius Pilate.

The Roman governor's face flushes and twists into an angry scowl. "What? Not again!" he explodes. "They got what they wanted – we crucified their 'King.' We broke the prisoners' legs. We're getting the bodies down before their ridiculous Sabbath. Tell him I've had enough of them today!"

"Excuse me, sir, but he's not one of the others. He's different – a member of their Council, but not one of those conspirators," explains the attendant. "He has a request concerning the burial of the preacher."

Pilate looks down at the marble floor for a moment, then up at his assistant. It's been a trying night, and he takes a moment to collect himself. "Alright, bring him in," he orders.

The man disappears down the hall and soon returns with a distinguished Jewish man wearing the robes of the Sanhedrin, the ruling council of the Jews, with which Pilate is more than familiar by this time.

"What is it you want?" asks Pilate abruptly.

"Most honorable governor, my name is Joseph, from the town of Arimathea," says the man, "and I am a member of the High Council of Israel. However, I am not among those who sought the death of the rabbi Jesus of Nazareth. And now, sir, I respectfully request that you allow me to take down the body of Jesus and give him a decent burial according to our customs."

Joseph speaks boldly, but with a note of kindness and reasonableness in his voice that impresses Pilate. The governor sees no reason to deny the request and says, "When he's dead, you may take the body and bury it as you wish."

Joseph says, "Sir, he is already dead."

"Already dead? Impossible! I just gave the order to break their legs!" exclaims the governor.

To the attendant he barks, "Send someone to fetch the centurion – immediately!"

He looks at Joseph and says, "Wait in the hallway."

Nearly a half hour passes.

The echo of footsteps jerks Joseph's head around. He watches as a Roman officer strides toward him, eyeing him without blinking. Only as the centurion turns and enters the governor's chamber does he take his icy stare from the Jewish elder.

Joseph inches toward the door to listen in on the conversation if he can.

"Yes, sir," the centurion is saying, "I was surprised, too. He died after only six hours. In fact . . ." he stops.

His eyes dart back and forth. With resolve, he starts again, "In fact, sir, he died just as the earthquake began. The whole experience was quite extraordinary . . . the darkness . . . the quake . . . the timing of his words . . . his strange attitude and manner . . . well, it was extraordinary, sir."

The governor breathes in deeply. "What is this? Don't tell me you've become a disciple of this preacher!"

"Oh, no, sir," replies the officer quickly. "No. I've been a Roman soldier for twenty years, and I've been in dozens of battles, seen thousands of men die. But all this was just too bizarre, I suppose. However, I have to admit this: if ever there was a 'Son of God,' something tells me this was he. But it doesn't really matter anyway, does it?

He's dead, and that's the end of that!"

"Well, it had *better* be the end of the matter," says Pilate. "It has fatigued both me and my wife. Is there any reason why the Jew in the hall shouldn't have the body for burial so we can get on with life around here?"

"None that I know of, sir," is the officer's response.

Joseph is recalled to the governor's presence and given permission to take the body of Jesus and bury it. So the elder rushes from the Fortress Antonia, out into the streets of Jerusalem. The sun is dipping low in the west, and already the buildings are glowing gold in the late afternoon light. Joseph knows the Sabbath is near – the sunset will usher in the Passover, and all activity in the streets will cease.

He finds his old friend, Nicodemus, also a member of the Council, and enlists his help. They devise their strategy: Nicodemus will quickly obtain the burial materials and meet Joseph at Golgotha. Meanwhile, Joseph will be removing Jesus from the cross, and together they will carry him to Joseph's own tomb nearby. They will quickly prepare the body for burial and try to rush back to the city before the start of the Sabbath.

It's agreed. Both men hurry off, their robes of respect flowing behind them.

Challenges

The crosses are casting long shadows as Joseph approaches the hill outside the gate. He has arrived only a minute or two after the centurion's return. The officer acknowledges him with a nod.

Only a handful of spectators remain now that sunset is near. Most of Jesus' disciples have drifted off in despair. Only the most faithful disciples and the most hateful enemies are still nearby.

With the help of some of the soldiers, Joseph lifts the cross of Jesus from its socket in the ugly hill and carefully lays it down. The nails are removed . . . Jesus is free from his terrible burden at last. In a real sense, he has been free from his burden since he closed his eyes and said, "It is finished."

The ordeal is over. Jesus has, in the words of the writer of Hebrews, "endured the cross, scorning its shame." And he has now entered into "the joy set before him" (Hebrews 12:2).

The cross was a challenge of obedience for Jesus. Again in the words of the Hebrews writer, "Although he was a son, he learned obedience from what he suffered and, once made perfect, he became the source of eternal salvation for all who obey him . . ." (Hebrews 5:8,9). The apostle Paul says that Christ Jesus "humbled himself and became obedient to [the point of] death – even death on a cross!" (Philippians 2:8).

The cross was his challenge of obedience. And don't we all have our challenges of obedience? In the events that surrounded the crucifixion, two other men were challenged: one succeeded in his test and one failed.

You remember Peter's challenge, don't you? He had said he would never forsake Jesus. But of course he did. The Lord actually prophesied that Peter would deny him three times on the night of the arrest. The way of the cross was Peter's challenge of obedience . . . and he failed. Just as Jesus had said, Peter denied he ever knew his Lord.

At the same time, however, Joseph of Arimathea met his challenge of obedience . . . and succeeded. In John 7:13, it says, regarding Jesus, "But no one would say anything publicly about him for fear of the Jews." And Joseph was one of those intimidated ones. He "was a disciple of Jesus, but secretly because he feared the Jews" (John 19:38).

Joseph was a pious man but also a man of position. He was a member of the most exclusive group among his people. In fact, he was at the pinnacle of his career; out of respect for his position, people stepped aside to allow him to pass on the street.

But when it came to the controversy over Jesus, Joseph had not consented to the decision and the action of the Sanhedrin when they condemned Jesus to death. Still, he knew that to be too closely associated with the popular preacher could cost him dearly in position, prestige and power.

Then came his challenge of obedience.

Mark makes two interesting and very revealing statements about Joseph. First, according to Mark, Joseph was "a prominent member of the Council, who was himself waiting for the kingdom of God . . ." (Mark 15:43). In a sense, Joseph is *waiting* for his moment of challenge . . . waiting for that special point of obedience, because he is expecting – anticipating – the rule of God to come on earth.

He listened carefully to Jesus' words, observed his life and became a secret disciple. Then he *waited.*

Unexpectedly, a crucial moment comes: Jesus has suffered and died at the hands of cruel men. Now he hangs shamefully on a cross outside (what used to be) God's holy city. Who will take down the Savior's body? Who will lay him to rest?

Mark also records a second bit of information about Joseph. He "went *boldly* to Pilate and asked for Jesus' body." Does Joseph think his bold action will go undetected, unnoticed by the Sanhedrin? He is no fool. He knows he will be bringing down the wrath of Jesus' enemies on himself. But this is his challenge of obedience, his moment of truth. And, to his everlasting credit, he obeys . . . and he is now immortalized in God's Word, as well as in God's heaven.

What about Peter? Peter failed his first real challenge, but the good news is, there were other challenges.

Forgiven by Jesus, Peter would go on to live a marvelous life for his Lord, successfully meeting many other challenges – until at last he too became "obedient to death."

But most of us know Peter's story. It is Joseph who is the man of the hour here near the end of the ordeal. It is Joseph who goes *boldly* to Pilate and goes *boldly* to Golgotha and will soon lay the Lord *boldly* in a tomb he had prepared for himself. He meets his challenge in a marvelous and most exemplary way.

Joseph knows the consequences of his bold action, but he chooses to obey – or perhaps, in a sense, he has no choice. He may feel he has no option but to do what he knows is right. Isn't it interesting that so many of Jesus' "friends" flee at the crucial moment? And it is the timid ones – the "secret disciples" – who rise to the occasion, who pass the acid test.

What's interesting is that Joseph and Nicodemus have much more to lose in openly supporting Jesus than the others. The apostles are fishermen, tax collectors, tradesmen from Galilee. But Jerusalem is "home turf" for Joseph and Nicodemus. They are leaders in their community, court justices for the whole Jewish nation. And they are in a tiny minority among their peers in the Sanhedrin. They're in jeopardy of losing everything.

Perhaps like Peter, we have failed in the past to meet a specific challenge of obedience, and it has left us shaken and ashamed. Think of forgiven Peter, who doesn't make the same mistake of denial again as new challenges come.

And from our brother Joseph of Arimathea, perhaps we can learn to wait for the kingdom. Wait for the challenge of obedience. And like him, we can seize the opportunity *boldly* when it finally comes, becoming obedient, even to the point of loss of position, prestige, power, possessions – and, if need be, the loss of our very lives.

Two Silhouettes At Sunset

The sun is very low now. The Sabbath is only a few minutes away – a half hour, three quarters of an hour at most. We stand at this step on the way to glory, staring at the terrible silhouettes on the hill. Three crosses . . . but the center cross is lifted, tilted back, finally laid on the ground.

Jesus is taken down. And that has monumental implications for the world. It's the signal that "it is finished." Jesus has paid the ransom for our release from the bondage of sin; he has satisfied the law's demands, the penalty of death we deserve. And we are free.

As he dies, we live. As he is taken down, we are lifted up to God.

At this moment, there are two silhouettes to which we are drawn here at Calvary. One is the Lord Jesus – spent, motionless, lifeless. The other is a man in the robes of an elder of Israel, gently cradling Jesus' body . . . filled with passion, fully alive for the first time. Joseph has been waiting all his life for the kingdom of God to come. Waiting. Waiting.

And now he has found it . . . in his arms.

Chapter Eleven

A BROKEN LOCK

"The soul's dark cottage, battered and decayed,
Lets in new light through chinks that Time has made;
Stronger by weakness, wiser, men become
As they draw near to their eternal home."

– Edmund Waller, 1686
On the Divine Poems

The small group of disciples is moving as quickly as it can with its precious burden. The body of Jesus has been wrapped in a blanket, and four men bear it on their shoulders. Joseph of Arimathea is leading the way to a small garden where there are several tombs, perhaps a hundred yards from the Place of the Skull.

Behind Joseph and the pallbearers is Nicodemus, who has arrived from the city with a large container filled with a mixture of myrrh and aloes. He is helped by another man, but the two of them struggle under the 75 pounds of spices.

Then, behind Nicodemus are some of the faithful women, especially Mary Magdalene and Mary the mother of Joses. They've come to see where Jesus will be laid. There may be opportunity for some of them to return after the Sabbath and tend to a more proper application of the grave clothes.

Off at a distance, there are suspicious and hate-filled eyes that watch the operation to ensure that Jesus is not heard from again.

The little procession arrives at its destination, and the garden is like a clear sky after a storm. The desolation, the smell of fear and suffering, the noises of evil deeds and the intimidating, pocked-faced Golgotha seem a thousand miles away. The place is quiet; shade trees lend their coolness to the gathering dusk – and screen from view the terrible place of the nightmare past.

"There!" says Joseph, looking back at those who are carrying Jesus. "Over there. I'll need some help with the stone."

They push the millstone-shaped rock back along the trough guide, and musty air rushes out of the dark tomb, along with wisps of dust stirred up by the earthquake. Inside, there is a niche carved into the wall of the small cave, cut flat on the bottom to form a ledge on which to lay the deceased.

Locked Away From Life

"Hurry, hurry!" urges Joseph as they lay Jesus' body on the ground near the tomb entrance. Immediately, two of the men grab the linen that has been brought along, and they begin tearing it into long strips. The ripping sound of the cloth seems to tear the fabric of silence in the garden as well. The raw sound is heard again and again as the pile of linen strips becomes a white mound next to Jesus' body.

Nicodemus opens the spice container, and instantly the fragrance overpowers the natural smell of the bushes and trees. Joseph kneels as Nicodemus dips the first linen strip into the container and holds it out.

Joseph pushes the sleeves of his elder's robe back, takes the strip from his colleague and wraps it around Jesus' feet. Almost in a single motion, he reaches for the next strip that dangles from Nicodemus' outstretched hand. With it he binds the upper feet and ankles together.

As quickly as they are able, the two distinguished Jewish elders wrap the body – the legs, the torso, the arms – then bind the arms to the chest. Finally, Joseph winds a strip around Jesus' neck . . . and stops.

He leans back on his knees and sits on his feet, looking deeply into the sadness frozen on the face of his master. "I'm old and ready to die," he is thinking, "but he was so young. What was he . . . 32, 33 years old? Too young to die! And we all had so much to learn from him. What will happen to us now?"

For the first time, tears roll down his craggy face, washing away his vision. He's overwhelmed with grief – as much for the nation of Israel as for their King. He sits looking down, not only at the death of the great teacher before him, but at the death of a wonderful dream. What has happened to the kingdom of God? It seemed so near . . . Joseph has waited so long, been disappointed so often.

His friend Nicodemus touches him gently on the shoulder then hands him a large piece of linen that will serve as the burial cloth for Jesus' face, and Joseph carefully lifts the head. Beginning underneath, he wraps the cloth around the head and across the face.

"It is done," he chokes. The spice and ointment mixture drips from his hands onto the ground, mingling with his tears. The younger men kneel, cradle the body, lift it together to waist height, and slowly move forward into the tomb. The pallbearers step down, bending to squeeze through the low, narrow entrance. Jesus is laid on the hard stone ledge, and the men climb back into the world of the living.

Now Joseph enters the tomb himself to see that all is in order. He stares down at the human yet nondescript cloth-covered shape before him. A single candle has been lit. It casts an almost strobe-like yellow light on the carved walls. The musty smell seems to relegate the place and its contents to the ancient past.

What is the distinguished elder thinking? Is he considering the strange turn of events that have put a once-vibrant young man on the stone death couch of an old man? Is he wondering how he can forgive his colleagues in the Sanhedrin for their blindness and blood-thirstiness? Is he resigning himself to never seeing the long-awaited kingdom of God? Or are the powerful yet gentle words of Jesus echoing through his mind?

With a short puff of breath he extinguishes the flame and steps back up into the garden. "Come, gentlemen, let's set the stone in place," he says with as much composure as he can muster.

The men lean their weight against the heavy stone wheel. It finally budges and moves slowly across the opening. The gritty, scraping sound of stone against stone becomes an eerie herald that the end has come, a brief chapter past.

Joseph looks toward the western sky. "It is the Sabbath," he announces. "We must return to our homes right away. Thank you all for your kindness. And may our beloved Teacher rest in peace."

The walk back into Jerusalem is fast-paced and silent. Each disciple is lost in thought. And behind the faithful are the shadowy figures of the haters of Jesus, ensuring that their enemy is dead and buried.

Throughout the city, across the land, in every home of every hamlet and town, Paschal lambs have been slaughtered – in memory of that ancient time in Egypt when the blood of the lamb, smeared on the posts and lintel of each Hebrew house, saved the faithful occupants from the passing death angel.

To a few tonight – to a very few – the significance of the moment will finally become evident. They will realize that the Passover sacrifice is a prophecy of the sacrificial death of Jesus. To a few, thoughts of the Paschal lamb will conjure up memories of a day, some three years ago, when John – the one they called "the baptizer" – looked up, saw Jesus and declared, "Behold, the Lamb of God who takes away the sin of the world!" (John 1:29).

A Vacancy

Christians since that time know that Jesus walked out of the grave on the third day after he was buried. But the disciples at that time didn't know the resurrection was coming. They should have known. Jesus had told them repeatedly what would happen . . . but somehow, they didn't listen.

Joseph was a rich man who was getting on in years. He had decided he wouldn't return to his hometown of Arimathea for his final days and his burial. After all, he had become a prominent member of the Sanhedrin in Jerusalem. His life was here – he would die here – he would be buried here. That was his decision, and just within the past few months, he had contracted with the stone cutters to carve out a tomb in the rock that bordered the pleasant little garden. There, in the shadow of the great wall of holy Jerusalem, he would be laid in his final resting place.

Then came the plot, the arrest, the trial and conviction and finally the execution of Jesus. Joseph was convinced that Jesus was teaching the truth, that he was, indeed, sent from Yahweh. He opposed those who were out to kill Jesus, but the young prophet had too many influential enemies.

Joseph went to Golgotha to see Jesus one last time. It was there that he discovered that most of Jesus' friends had fled. Who would take him down from the cross and give him a decent burial? Somehow, Joseph knew that God had placed that burden – that incomparable privilege! – on him.

So he gave his newly carved tomb to his young friend

and master. He undoubtedly thought he was giving it to him forever. What a shocking and joyous surprise was in store for faithful Joseph in just a day and a half or so! Jesus walked out of the tomb – leaving a vacancy! Which gives rise to an intriguing question: What happened to Joseph's tomb after the resurrection? The only reasonable answer I can give is that *Joseph used it.* A tomb so fine and so near to the great city of Jerusalem would not simply be left empty, nor would anyone fill it back up with rock or earth. And it seems most unlikely that it would be sold to another after Jesus had laid there. It seems evident to me that Joseph himself used his tomb in the way it was intended . . . for his own eventual burial.

Christians speak of "the empty tomb." It's the symbol of a great theological truth. And true enough, the grave was empty on that third day after the crucifixion. But shall we believe it remained empty forever?

There's no reason why the elder wouldn't use his own tomb for the purpose for which he had purchased it. And thus the thrilling thought: some time later (perhaps a year or two or five or ten) Joseph died and was laid in his tomb . . . which also was *the tomb of Jesus*! The old disciple was placed in the niche where Jesus was placed; they shared the same stone death couch.

Somehow the thought boggles my mind! To lie in death at *exactly* the place where Jesus was laid!

Once the resurrection was a fact, did it give Joseph comfort to know that he would occupy the same tomb as Jesus? I believe the great elder knew very well that if the hole in the rock couldn't contain his Lord, it couldn't contain him either.

Just think of being buried in the tomb that Christ broke open! What an honor to have one's body placed where the Savior was placed; but even more, what *confidence* one would find there in that "broken" tomb. It's like being "locked" in a cell that has a broken lock.

Death and the grave were conquered by Jesus, and, through him, the one who lies in his place also will conquer death and the grave.

Now consider that *every* tomb is the tomb of Jesus, and *every* grave has been broken by him – whether in a hillside cemetery, on the plain, in the ocean, or scattered across the wasteland – *every* grave is his. He's been there. He shared the experience, shared all our graves . . . he *broke* all our graves. And we shall walk out of them one day as surely as he did. Praise God!

A Hum of Cosmic Force

The garden is quiet now. And dark. For, the Sabbath night has settled softly over Jerusalem and the Judean hills.

Beyond the high wall, in the city, thousands of inhabitants are celebrating. They're gathered in comfortable homes, are seated around tables spread with the various foods that memorialize that night centuries ago when Moses and the Israelites prepared to escape their Egyptian slavery.

Overhead, an inky sky is punctured with pinpoints of light. And outside the city walls, the dark garden is as lonely now as it was refreshing earlier. The heat of the day has evaporated into the chill of the night.

Pull your coat tighter and stand with me here. This place of flowers, shrubs and trees, is also a place of dead men's bones. And that thought seems to make the place more unfriendly.

But Jesus is here. Behind the large disk of stone there against the rocky hill. He lies lifeless. He's not sleeping, not in a coma. He is dead.

As we stand here in the darkness, I suggest that you and I, in spirit, offer Jesus our own graves. Because the time is coming when you and I – when everyone – will breathe out and not breathe in. We will take our places in some kind of grave – in the ground, in an urn, in a mausoleum, in the sea, or scattered to the winds.

Wherever death takes us, let us here and now, at this step on the way to glory, give our death places to Jesus Christ. No matter how frightening, he will take it and break it, just as he did for Joseph of Arimathea. And a broken tomb can't hold the faithful for very long.

But right now, the garden is dark and lonely, and we're a bit nervous – a little fearful. Is that the creaking of the city gate, or is it the cackling of Satan as he relishes his supposed victory over Jesus? Is that snapping sound only a little ground squirrel, or is it the enemies of Jesus spying on us, lying in wait for us?

Maybe it's time for us to go back to the city, too. Maybe we can find some friendly faces there, far from this place of dead men's bones.

The way of the cross already seems like a bad dream: Jesus condemned, carrying his cross, falling, meeting his mother; Simon pressed into service; Jesus speaking to the women, stripped of his garments, nailed to the cross . . . dying . . . taken down . . . buried in a borrowed tomb. The Fortress Antonia, the Via Dolorosa, the city gate, even the horrible Place of the Skull now seem far away, long ago.

For some people, this is the end. To them the way of the cross leads here – to the tomb – and no further. But for those who believe, the way of the cross leads home to glory . . . to God the Father.

The silence of the garden is intimidating in some ways. But there's no sense of finality in the air this Sabbath night. Instead, if we are attuned, we can feel a tension, a faint sense of anticipation. A hum of cosmic force. A distant vibration before the quake of all time . . . .

Jesus is laid in the tomb. But not for long.

Chapter Twelve

POWER IN THE MORNING

"Morning has broken
Like the first morning,
Blackbird has spoken
Like the first bird.
Praise for the singing!
Praise for the morning!
Praise for them, springing
Fresh from the Word!"

– Eleanor Farjeon, 1931

In the eastern sky, the stars haven't quite fled away. The earliest fingers of dawn only brush the horizon as they prepare to push back the night.

Listen! From a nearby bush comes the first chirp of an enterprising bird who dares to break the nocturnal silence. He's joined by another anxious greeter of the morning. It won't be long before a feathery chorus will offer an anthem of praise to the Creator of the sunrise.

But for now, torches still illuminate the little garden outside the wall, casting distorted shadows of the guards against the rocky slope and into the mottled shapes of the shrubs and trees. The Jewish leaders had insisted on a guard, because they remembered Jesus saying he would rise again on the third day.

The strange dancing shadows are only illusions that give motion to the motionless guards whose eyes are heavy with sleep. Indeed, some have succumbed to the stillness, the boredom, the uneventful night and have drifted into slumber. Others, aware of their duty – even the preposterous duty of guarding a dead man's grave –

are fighting the overwhelming urge to slip into the release of dreamless sleep.

Now the faintest eastern light tiptoes into the torch-lit garden, dimly outlining the great round stone that covers the tomb in the rock. As it does, the night bird stops her singing.

She hears something! She *feels* something!

It begins as a low rumble, like the sound of a 100-car freight train coming from a distance – moving fast, racing toward us at breakneck speed. A second later, there's a vibration . . . then the solid earth begins to move from side to side. Finally it rolls with violent jolts.

Another earthquake! A *true* aftershock!

Instantly, every guard is wide awake with fear, most of them on all fours, trying to ride out the quake. Then the rumbling moves off into the distance. The shaking stops. It's quiet once more.

A few seconds elapse. Then there's a sound that sends shivers down the back of every guard – terror into every heart. It's a raspy, gritty, scraping sound that is completely discordant to the quiet of the garden – discordant even to the distant thunder of the quake that still reverberates in the minds of the guards.

The large stone that covers the tomb entrance is moving! . . . slowly rolling backward along the trough . . . on its own! No hands touch it, no shoulders are bent against it. It moves under the invisible control of an overpowering spiritual presence. The grinding of rock against rock scrapes away the sensibilities of the guards, and they become as dead men.

With a heavy thud, the huge round stone reaches the end of the trough and halts. After another moment, a shape – a person – slips silently up the hewn steps into the garden . . . and is gone.

But before we witness the conclusion of this astounding scene, let's step back a few hours . . .

A Fitful Night

It's Saturday evening; about 24 hours have passed since the hurried burial. Joseph and Nicodemus and the others had quickly carried Jesus to the nearby garden, wrapped him in linen strips soaked in spice and ointment, laid him in the tomb in the rock and rolled the heavy stone cover across the doorway. They had raced against the descending sun, for the Passover Sabbath began at sunset.

Now it's sunset on Saturday. The Sabbath – the seventh day – is ending, and the first day of the week is beginning. (Remember, in the Jewish accounting of time, the day begins at sunset and ends at the next sunset – as in Genesis, "The evening and the morning were the first day . . . .") With the Holy Day concluded, merchants are again selling their wares, so Mary Magdalene and the other women rush out into the evening to buy spices (Mark 16:1). Their intention is to return to the grave when morning comes and give a more careful burial preparation to Jesus' body. To be sure, they appreciate the efforts of Joseph and Nicodemus. But the rushed embalming is not appropriate for the Lord, in their view.

They return to the house of a friend with the cloth and spices and wait for the first light. We can be certain that their sleep is fitful. How can they sleep peacefully when the Lord has been crucified? How can they ever be at peace again?

Mary Magdalene awakens with a start from her pallet on the floor. She has lost track of how many times her sleep has been interrupted. Visions of the horrible day, only a few hours past, haunt her rest – visions of the Lord dragging his heavy cross, being nailed to it, hanging between heaven and earth . . . dying . . . dying.

Finally, she can lie there no longer. She gets up, rolls the pallet and sets it aside. Then she begins preparing the burial spices. It's still dark outside; dawn is perhaps an hour or more away.

Now, one by one, the other women rise. They, too, have been unable to sleep soundly. Quietly, they finish the preparations, pull on their cloaks and step out into the darkness. They file into the empty street: first, faithful Mary of Magdala, then Mary the mother of James, Salome, Joanna, and the others.

They walk silently, carefully, guided by the lamps that several of them have brought. Suddenly, they hear the rumbling sound – the same one that stops the bird's song in the garden. The earth begins to roll and quake! The women freeze in fear. They fall to the cobblestoned street. Then, as quickly as it began, it's over.

Lamps are coming on in every house along the street. People are beginning to peer out of their shuttered windows into the pre-dawn. Mary Magdalene is filled with anticipation – not joyous expectation – but an impatience and agitation, like a prisoner who's been locked away for a long time and now is ready to run, escape.

She turns to her companions. "I'm going ahead," she says in a low voice. "It will be light soon. I want to see if the earthquake has disturbed the tomb. Mary and I saw where they buried the Lord, so she can guide you to the place. I must hurry!"

A Shocking Discovery

The pent-up energy, frustration and pain are somehow channeled to her legs, and Mary's quick pace turns into a trot. Holding her lamp out in front of her as she quickly moves along, she rounds a corner and glances toward the east. There's still a starry canopy overhead, but the eastern sky has gone from ebony to cobalt to royal blue. A sliver of moonlight faintly outlines the city gate looming ahead.

The huge gate is still closed, but she petitions the

wary guard, who opens the small side-door and allows her to slip through. The smooth cobblestones of the city give way to the dirt and gravel of the road.

She shivers as she passes the ghostly shape of Golgotha. In the semi-darkness she can't quite make out the gouges that look like skull eye-sockets, but she can imagine them glaring at her, laughing at her, watching her every step. She realizes that she has slowed to a walk, and the dark skull spurs her into a run.

The garden is very close now. "Must slow down," she pants, " . . . guards will think someone's attacking them!"

Her lungs are heaving. She hasn't run so far and so fast since she was a girl growing up along the southwestern banks of the Sea of Galilee. In the blink of an eye, she is thinking of home and Magdala – of a little girl at play, then of a young women who became caught up in an evil life, a life that somehow eventually allowed seven demons into her spirit.

"Then he came that day," she remembers with a gentle smile, "and touched me – and the demons fled out of me screaming . . . and I looked at him and saw that wonderful face . . . ."

In an instant, the sunlit face in her mind evaporates, replaced by the tortured face of the crucified Jesus. Tears well up in her eyes for the hundredth time; she blinks and the night wind carries them away.

It's becoming lighter by the second now, but still she holds her lamp high, waves it slightly to signal the guards. "Hello!?" she cries out to the men. And again, "Hello! Is anyone there?"

A few more steps and she's in the garden. To her dismay, the guards are sitting, slumped again the rocks, quietly shaking, staring as if dead or in a trance. They don't respond to her voice. It's as if she's invisible to them.

Fear grips her heart. She glances in the direction of the tomb where, a day and a half earlier, she watched them bury Jesus. She sets her lamp on the ground abruptly.

The stone is rolled back; the grave is wide open, like the gaping, black yawn of some stone monster!

"What is happening?" she exclaims. "What's happened to the guards?" With the tomb open, she assumes the worst. "And who has taken away the Lord?"

The faint glow of the new day is tinting the east as she races from the garden with a jumble of thoughts tumbling in her head. "Who has done this terrible thing? Wasn't it enough that they crucified him? But why would anyone want to take away his body – what possible good would it do anyone? Must tell Peter and the others! Or . . . could it be *they* who have carried him away? No! They're afraid to even show their faces in the streets. Then . . . who?"

She runs south, toward a different city gate, taking a shortcut to the house where the disciples are hiding. A nervous guard opens the gate and lets Mary slip into the city as dawn warms the dark canopy above.

Finally, out of breath, she arrives at the house and knocks on the door. After a few moments, she impatiently pounds again. A nervous voice on the other side calls out, "Who . . . who's there?"

"It's me, Mary! I must see Simon Peter immediately!"

A bolt slides back, the door creaks open, she steps inside. Wide eyes beneath tousled hair stare at her in dull puzzlement. Peter stands. John is nearby.

"What is it, Mary?" they say simultaneously. "What's wrong?"

"They have taken away the Lord out of the tomb," she says, "and we do not know where they have laid him" (John 20:2).

Do Not Be Afraid

The other women have now reached the garden, which by this time is bathed in rose-colored, early morning light. The whispered topic of discussion is, "Who will roll away the stone for us from the entrance to the tomb?" (Mark 16:3).

Mary the mother of Joses is in the lead. She gasps, then shouts, "Look!" The others follow the direction of her index finger to the rocky slope and the open grave. They look in amazement at the huge round stone that has been moved along the trough, exposing the entrance to the tomb.

Only now do they realize that the guards are still present, in a sort of stupor, with glazed eyes and mouths gaping. The frightened women slip silently past the guards to the tomb entrance. Mary the mother of James steps down into the tomb; the others nervously crowd in behind her.

Though it's early dawn, the women's lamps are still lit, and the light illuminates the inside of the cramped cave. Immediately they look at one another with wide eyes – someone else is present! They can't see the body of Jesus, but from nowhere two men appear – so close they can reach out and touch them. The men's robes are dazzling white, like the morning sun, difficult to look at directly.

The terrified women fall to the stone floor and bow their faces low (Luke 24:5). One of the angels whispers, "Do not be afraid; for I know that you are looking for Jesus the Nazarene who has been crucified."

The other angel gently says, "Why do you seek the living One among the dead? He is not here, for he has risen just as He said. Remember how He spoke to you while He was still in Galilee, saying that the Son of Man must be delivered into the hands of sinful men, and be crucified, and the third day rise again" (Luke 24:5-7).

Then the first angel says, "Come, see the place where He was lying. And go quickly and tell His disciples that He has risen from the dead and behold, He is going before you into Galilee, there you will see Him; behold, I have told you" (Matthew 28:6,7).

The trembling women scramble through the narrow door and up into the garden. They cling to one another in fear, and yet the fear is mingled with indescribable joy in their footsteps as they rush back toward the city.

Mary Returns

There's a stirring in the garden. The guards look around with panic and disbelief in their eyes. They've been there in the garden all through the astounding events, in a deathly trance, and now they're violently shaking and jabbering like wild men. "What shall we do?" they cry.

They were set as a watch over the tomb, prepared for any eventuality. But the tomb is wide open – Jesus is gone. How can they explain it to their superiors? How can they explain it to themselves?

They decide that the chief priests must be told immediately, despite the punishment they as guards might receive. (Remember that these are temple guards, not Roman soldiers.) So some of them run toward the temple courts where the Sanhedrin meets. The rest remain behind to *guard the empty grave!* (Matthew 28:11).

Only moments after the women have rushed to tell the disciples of the strange happenings (followed by the dispatching of some of the guards to inform the high priest), there's the sound of running footsteps. John bursts into the garden, causing the skittish guards to stumble backward with a clatter.

John pauses, glances at the guards, scans the garden until he see the tomb entrance and rushes to it. He pulls up abruptly, stoops and peers inside. By the dim light of dawn, he can make out the linen wrappings on the death couch. Meanwhile, Peter arrives, breathing heavily as he tries to keep up with his younger companion.

He quickly moves to where John is gazing down into the tomb, shoulders him aside, and bounds down into the cave in the rock. Peter's eyes widen as he sees the linen burial wrappings, still heavy with spice and ointment, lying on the ledge in the niche . . . as if the body inside had evaporated!

But what is even stranger, the burial cloth that had been wrapped around Jesus' head is rolled neatly and sitting by itself on the ledge (John 20:7). Peter stares down at it in bewilderment. He feels a hand on his shoulder – John has ventured down into the tomb with him. Together they ponder the possibilities. Could it be . . . could it be that *he's alive*? Or did someone steal the body of the Lord? Who would stand to profit if Jesus' body disappeared? Were the Jews intending to humiliate the disciples by parading the body through the streets? These and other thoughts pour through their minds.

"Let's get back and report to the others," Peter says.

Both men quickly climb the few steps back to the garden. In deep thought, they run down the path to the road, passing near Mary Magdalene who has followed them. But in their bewilderment, they don't even acknowledge her presence.

Mary watches the two disciples go. Their pace is swift, but their shoulders are slumped. She wonders why they didn't notice her, and suddenly she feels very alone.

Now she is drawn to the tomb. She stands in front of it with the radiant morning light streaming across her face. But the beauty and freshness of the morning is lost to her. In fact, she's never felt so lost herself. Never felt so alone. So empty.

Her small frame shakes with silent sobs. Her only real friend has been torn from her, tearing her heart in two at the same time. Now she has been cheated of the opportunity of saying farewell to him, of expressing her devotion and adoration by cleansing his body of the dried blood and grit, of gently applying the fresh spices and wrapping him in clean linen.

She thinks again of the day Jesus entered her life. She had been used by people, made to feel like a "thing," less than human. She despised herself, gave herself increasingly to evil. "If I'm not a valuable person," she may have reasoned, "then I'll act accordingly. I'll become less than human, without natural affections – without conscience."

Then the demons came like slick hucksters, inching their way into her heart and soul, saying the lies she wanted to hear. Not only was she used by people, she also was used by evil spirits as a fleshly receptacle, a physical tool of the Evil One.

But Jesus came that certain day, and he looked into her soul – saw the true Mary buried beneath the ugliness of the intrusive spirits. He commanded the demons to leave her. And they obeyed! She was reborn. She was loved. She was a person of worth.

The Teacher Lives!

"Somehow, I expect him to be lying there on that stone ledge – as if I had overlooked him," she thinks, bending over once more to peer into the tomb.

Suddenly her heart pounds wildly! There are two men inside the tomb!

"Impossible!" she thinks. "Simon Peter and John just walked away – they left an empty tomb behind!"

Her knees are weak. Her legs shake, begin to give way as she notices the men's glowing robes. They are messengers from God! It's the only explanation, she concludes. And they are sitting at either end of the niche where Jesus was laid (John 20:12).

"Woman, why are you crying?" one of the angels calls out.

Her trembling voice barely answers, "They have taken my Lord away . . . and, and I don't know where they have put him."

As compelling as the two figures are before her, Mary senses that someone is behind her. She's sure of it. She quickly glances back to see a man standing just a few feet away.

"Woman, why are you crying?" the man asks. "Who is it you are looking for?"

She looks at him for a moment. His face is partly in the shadow cast by the hood of his cloak. "He must be the caretaker of the garden, just arriving at work," she thinks. "Maybe he knows where they have taken my Lord."

She clears her throat and weakly speaks. "Sir, if you have carried him away, tell me where you have put him, and I will get him."

Silence.

Then just a word from beneath the hood.

"Mary . . . ."

Something like 10,000 volts shoots through her, from her head to her feet! From her mind to her soul! All the warmth and security she has known in the presence of the Lord Jesus Christ come rushing in like a sweet flood of wildflowers.

The hood falls back. It is he.

"Teacher!" she cries out.

In one great leap, Mary is at his feet, her arms wrapped tightly around his legs – holding him so close that, she hopes, he will never be taken away again. Her face is bathed in tears, the garden echoes with sobs of joy.

Strong hands slip gently onto her shoulders and lift her up. That familiar voice gently says, "Do not hold on to me, for I have not yet returned to the Father. Go instead to my brothers and tell them, 'I am returning to my Father and your Father, to my God and your God'" (John 20:17).

With that, he withdraws his hands from her shoulders, looks deeply into her eyes with an unspoken message of assurance, turns slowly and walks away. Mary's heart seems ready to burst with happiness and excitement. Her body is charged with tremendous energy, and she races toward the house where she found the disciples earlier.

Travelers and eager merchants are just beginning to move along the road in the crisp, morning air as the woman sprints by like an Olympic runner. Her robe and cloak stream behind her . . . there is wild abandon in her long strides. Joy surges through her like a miracle serum. Morning has broken . . . like the first morning . . .

And we join her, matching her stride for stride. For we feel the power, too . . . the glorious power of the resurrection of our Master, our friend . . .

Praise God! Jesus is risen! He is risen, indeed!

Epilogue

REMEMBERING THE GLORY

"O what their joy and their glory must be,
Those endless sabbaths the blessed ones see!"

– Peter Abelard (1079-1142)
Hymnus Paraclitensis

The risen Savior will appear to many people over the course of the next forty days. The apostle Paul will one day write ". . . he appeared to Peter, and then to the Twelve. After that, he appeared to more than five hundred of the brothers at the same time, most of whom are still living, though some have fallen asleep. Then he appeared to James, then to all the apostles . . . ."

These appearances occur before Jesus returns to the Father. But Paul will testify that the Lord Jesus makes at least one more appearance in future years. At the same passage, Paul adds, ". . . and last of all he appeared to me also, as to one abnormally born" (1 Corinthians 15:5-7).

The resurrection isn't a shadowy thing, a midnight ghost story. Jesus walks out of the tomb just before dawn, and his first appearance is in the crystal light of morning.

And to whom does he give the honor of seeing his risen body for the first time? To Peter or John? To Andrew or James or to the other great pillars of the church?

Mark records it for all time: "When Jesus rose early on the first day of the week, he appeared first to Mary Magdalene, out of whom he had driven seven demons" (Mark 16:9).

From a despised, demon-possessed wretch to the beloved first witness of the resurrected Lord of Life! That's a picture of the grace of God! That's where the way of the cross leads . . . to glory! Glory for the suffering Savior, glory for all who walk the way with him – even the most wretched of believers.

In one sense, it has been a long journey – from the shameful judgment hall and the torturous Via Dolorosa to the deadly Place of the Skull . . . and the tomb that was broken. But in another sense, it has been a matter of only 48 hours or so.

This journey is at the very heart of Christianity. There's wonder in the incarnation of the Son of God. There's amazement in the miracles, in the healings of the Great Physician. There's wisdom and life in the words of the Master Teacher. But the salvation and hope of every Christian is purchased during these 48 hours, on this journey. They are the most crucial hours in the history of the world.

That's why we must return again and again to walk the way of the cross. The entire way. Not just a quick courtesy call at Calvary on the way to Easter. Indeed, our hope comes through the resurrection – but our salvation comes through the cross – and the cross begins, not at Golgotha, but at the judgment hall of Pontius Pilate.

As we return to walk this way again, each place of reflection will become more meaningful, more precious, more holy to us – not because we earn some kind of currency in God's grace, but because our appreciation of his free gift is deepened by meditating on the tremendous cost to the Giver. At each step, God will reveal new insights, new lessons for life. The way to glory will bring us back to the center of our faith and existence.

Join me in memory once more at the garden tomb. Remember our sister Mary of Magdala running like the wind with the greatest news the world has ever known. He lives! The way has been opened to God's heaven!

But don't forget where he walked, where you and I walked . . . through the valley of the shadow of death . . . in the way of the cross.

And never forget that, even though the way of the cross is the long way home, it is the only way that truly leads to glory.

NOTES

For those who want to know more about the Way of the Cross

The practice of walking the devotional way of the cross may date back to the earliest centuries of the Christian era. It is believed that faithful Christians far removed from the Holy Land may have used a series of reflection points as a substitute for the pilgrimages they were unable to make to the places hallowed by Jesus Christ.

There are those who believe that the custom originated from the tradition that, after the ascension of the Lord, Jesus' mother, Mary, went back to visit various places along the route Jesus took to the cross. And that is believed to be the beginning of what, to this day, is known as the "Via Dolorosa" or Way of Sorrows in Jerusalem.

Visitors to the city today can walk through the streets of the section called the "Old City" and see the various historical points marked by plaques or other depictions on the walls of buildings. It also is likely that visitors will see pilgrims walking along Jesus' route as they have done for centuries, stopping at each of the places of reflection. Of course, many believe that the original street that Jesus walked is twenty or more feet below the present street – because of the repeated destruction of Jerusalem over the years and the rebuilding of the city on the ruins of the earlier structures.

Most Roman Catholic churches have a series of pictures or small sculpted scenes, called "the Stations of the Cross," along the side walls of the sanctuary. At times, faithful Catholics walk from Station to Station, often accompanied by a priest who leads the devotional thoughts, pausing at each Station to meditate on the particular event on the way of the cross represented by the depiction.

In addition, the Stations of the Cross are set out along pathways in a number of religious retreat centers across America and around the world. Those retreats, like Serra Retreat in Malibu, California, are often operated by the Order of the Friars Minor – the Franciscan Fathers.

Perhaps the earliest coherently related Stations outside Palestine were those erected at the church of San Stefano in Bologna, Italy, during the 5th century.

Private devotion using the Stations of the Cross became somewhat more widespread in the 12th and 13th centuries as returning Crusaders set up tableaux (striking, dramatic scenes or pictures) at home to represent various places in the Holy Land where they had been. We can imagine how those "soldiers of the cross" who risked their lives to "liberate" the places made holy by Jesus' very presence would cherish the Via Dolorosa – how they would want to walk it in memory. During those centuries, the tableaux and the devotion centered around them were known as "the Little Jerusalem."

But it was the 15th century before the concept of the Stations of the Cross became a general practice. Even then, it was practiced only in monasteries, friary chapels and churches that the Franciscan Fathers served throughout the world. The Franciscans had taken over custody of the "holy places" in 1342. As a part of that mission, they believed it their duty not only to care for the holy places, but also to promote devotion to those places – among which, of course, were the Via Dolorosa, Calvary (Golgotha), the garden tomb and other locations that relate to the Passion of Christ. So in the following centuries, they were successful in expanding the devotion to the Stations of the Cross.

Paul Jerome Casanova (1676-1751), who eventually became known as St. Leonard of Port Maurice, spent much of his life promoting devotion to the Stations. In fact, he was so enthusiastic and successful in his mission that he became known as the "preacher of the Way of the Cross."

Since the concept of the devotion began as random, personal worship, understandably there was great diversity in the number and titles of the Stations in the early centuries. For example, in 5th century Bologna, there were only five Stations of the Cross. In Antwerp, there were seven. And at various times, individuals proposed and participated in twenty, thirty or more Stations. In these different versions, the proposed number of times Jesus fell along the Via Dolorosa, for example, varied from one to seven.

One particular Station that is included in the official Catholic practice of today, but that is of much later development, is the tradition that a woman named Veronica met Jesus on the way to the cross and wiped his face with her veil. Although it's a very beautiful thought, to my knowledge there's no early evidence for this happening.

Regarding procedure, it seems logical to most of us that if we were to follow the steps of Jesus, we would begin at the judgment hall or even Gethsemane and proceed along the way to the cross. However, for many centuries, the stations were often set in reverse order, with people beginning at Calvary and retracing Jesus' steps back to the place of judgment.

The number of Stations of the Cross that is official in the Roman Catholic Church today is fourteen, that number first appearing in manuals of devotion published in the 16th century. The determination of that particular number seems to be based more on the choice of devotional writers than on the actual practice of pilgrims in Jerusalem visiting the holy places. The Catholic Church later simply confirmed the tradition that had developed over time, and the fourteen stations became standard practice.

In this book I chose to visit twelve halting places rather than the official number of the Catholic Church. I hope you understood why I decided to delete three of the fourteen and to add one which they don't include.

The accepted Stations of the Cross in the Roman Catholic Church today are:

1. Christ is condemned to death by Pilate
2. Jesus is made to carry the cross
3. Jesus falls the first time
4. Jesus meets His blessed Mother
5. The cross is laid on Simon of Cyrene
6. Veronica wipes the face of Jesus
7. Jesus falls the second time
8. Jesus speaks to the women of Jerusalem
9. Jesus falls the third time
10. Jesus is stripped of His garments and receives gall to drink
11. Jesus is nailed to the cross
12. Jesus dies on the cross
13. Jesus is taken down from the cross
14. Jesus is laid in the sepulcher

Some have proposed a 15th Station: the resurrection

of the Lord (the one I added). Indeed, many modern Catholic theologians and liturgists emphasize that Christ's death should not be dissociated from his resurrection. There are Catholics who believe that devotion to the way of the cross is psychologically and theologically incomplete if it ends at the cross rather than at the resurrection.

In 1686, Pope Innocent XI granted Franciscans and those affiliated with them the same indulgences that could be gained by making an actual, personal pilgrimage to the Holy Land and to the actual places on the way of the cross. This is where most Protestants would have to part company with Catholics, even if they see the value in the devotional practice. It was the theology of granting and even selling indulgences, you will remember, that set a Catholic priest named Martin Luther to studying the whole matter of salvation by faith and grace – and the eventual religious division between German Catholics and Protestants.

Still, I firmly believe God *will* grant grace, if not indulgences, to the penitent soul who seeks to journey, step by step, with the Lord on his painful yet glorious way to the cross. I don't envision that grace as some kind of heavenly currency with which we can buy or bribe our way into heaven. Jesus has already paid the price of our entrance into God's presence, once and for all. And on our part, that entrance is assured through faith.

Rather, I believe God grants peace, assurance, increased faith, hope and other qualities summed up by the word "grace" to every believer who devotes himself or herself to the Lord – in whatever devotional exercise is chosen. For me, this particular exercise is exceptionally powerful and graceful for the reasons which I hope have become apparent as you read the book.

I believe that, as Christians, we often venture deep into the faith, endeavoring to plumb the depths of God's

Word. We diligently study the writings of Paul, Peter, John, James . . . seeking to understand how those ancient directions given to the early church might apply to us in our contemporary world.

As we struggle with the Epistles for prolonged times, however, we can drift away from the simplicity and power of the original words of Jesus in the gospels. And we can lose sight of the most significant thing in the faith of Jesus Christ – the way of the cross.

I'm not suggesting that we have actually *forgotten* that Jesus died on a cross. Many of our hymns, sermons, prayers and Bible lessons affirm that fact – over and over again. But I am suggesting that it is easy to give a nodding affirmation to the fact of the cross without contemplating, *meditating*, on the reality of the cross and the resurrection – from start to finish.

I have tried to emphasize the concept of *identification* rather than merely *affirmation*. For example, it is far different to visit and comfort a Christian brother or sister in the hospital than to merely acknowledge that he or she is ill and hospitalized. The difference is *being there*.

My prayer is that we will revisit the Way of Sorrows again and again – walking with Jesus, feeling his pain and shame, going "outside the camp" to him (see Hebrews 13:11-14), outside our comfort zones – and of course, also revisit the empty grave, with all its hope and exultation.

The reason identification is so vital is that the more we are *with* Jesus, the more we will become *like him*. The way of the cross is his supreme moment, the moment we must share with him repeatedly. It will humble us. And it will change us through the power of the indwelling Spirit of God.

May we determine to know nothing but Jesus Christ crucified and raised from the dead.